LOVE RISES
A POST-BELLUM ROMANCE
by
Bella Battle

COPYRIGHT

This is a work of fiction. Names, characters, places, events, and incidents are either products of the author's imagination or used fictitiously, and any resemblances to actual persons, living or dead, business establishments, events, or locales is entirely coincidental.

DEDICATION

This book is dedicated to all my Southern relatives, living or dead, and especially to that long ago president of the University of Texas at Austin who recorded our family history.

ACKNOWLEDGMENTS

Thanks to my family up North headed by Mab and John, and special thanks to Lyn and Steve, Jeanne and Jay, who encourage and facilitate my life and my writing. Also, to Gerardo, my wonderful tech guy and friend, to Carl, Terry, and all the Lesser North Texas Writers who give their time and expertise to making all of us better writers. I would be remiss if I did not include Jim Morris, great encourager from long ago.

PROLOGUE

THE AMERICAN CIVIL WAR BEGAN IN 1861 AND ENDED IN 1865. THE NORTH/SOUTH BATTLE CALLED RECONSTRUCTION, RAGED ON UNTIL 1877.

Ripped from a slow and sleepy life of mint juleps on the veranda and bountiful crops of cotton, the little town of Washington, Georgia was thrust into a bloody civil war followed by a violent aftermath called Reconstruction. During these terrible years, the rural town's architecture had remained intact since upper Georgia was outside the path of Sherman's March to the Sea. Still, Washington's outlying plantations were stripped either by Southern troops or Union soldiers, and there was no one left to plant or harvest. A few former slaves remained with plantation owners by choice or because they did not know how to survive without the plantation structure. Their presence served only to stretch already meager supplies.

Charles Irving of the Irving Guards, General Robert Augustus Toombs and his wife Julia, often referred to as the most beautiful woman in the South, lived and loved during this continuing turmoil. Along with most Southerners, they thought restoring self-government could revive their way of life. These three were more than willing to break taboos of the old South and do whatever was necessary to rid their land of Yankees.

The Union was certain that restoration of the South's lifestyle would establish another form of slavery for freedmen to endure. Union troops were as determined to crush the South and its leadership as Southerners were to fight until Northern forces withdrew.

Political reshaping of the South, bought with violence and tenacity by Ex-Rebels in most southern states, was a silent victory.

Even though removal of the military has always signaled defeat, withdrawal of Union troops from the South went largely unreported in northern newspapers in 1877.

Love Rises

Significant stories are often best told by details of the lives of those who were there at the beginning. After any war, neither side can accurately predict the future and the changes it will bring. What happened to Charlie, Julia, and General Toombs in this story would not have happened in ordinary times.

Chapter 1
Escape

Washington, Georgia, May, 1865

The young lieutenant burst through the heavy door into the Toombs' mansion. "General! General!" he shouted. "We have only a few minutes. Union troops are on their way to arrest you."

The General heard Charlie at the door and made it halfway down the stairs before he bellowed, "Gray Alice is tethered behind the house. Let's move. By God, if standing by the state of Georgia is treason, then I'm guilty."

Julia Toombs, her long black curls in disarray, appeared on the stairs behind her husband, pulling her red velvet sleeve up over one shoulder.

Charlie and Julia stole a moment to exchange a silent message. Something passed between them that had nothing to do with treason or escape. Lieutenant Charles Irving stood almost at attention. His stiff body belied the yearning in his eyes as he looked at Julia. *Her eyes are heavy with emotion. Have I misread her? Is that just a look of concern for her husband? If only she hadn't turned those liquid brown eyes on me. Is she as attracted to me as I am to her? What a treacherous bastard I am to think of betraying my General, even in my imagination.*

General Toombs turned to embrace his wife and kiss her goodbye. "I'll send you word from Roanoke," he said as he released her. "Dear God, how I hate to leave you alone in these perilous times."

"I'll be fine," Julia said. "Take care, both of you," she added, emphasizing the word *both.*

"Please, General, there is no time," Charlie pled.

As the two moved through the kitchen and approached the back steps, it was as though the older man had just lost a battle; his head down, his gait slow, his body radiating defeat. He crossed the back porch and looked down at the steps as if descent was too daunting. Raising his head, he spoke to Charlie. "I can't leave her, Charlie. I can't leave Julia." Even his voice was broken. "A man shouldn't be driven out of his home, away from his wife. It's not natural."

The General had long required his lieutenant to carry liquor for him. In an accustomed gesture, Charlie whipped a small, silver flask from his pocket and handed it to his superior who drank the whiskey like it was a lifeline. "Nothing about war is natural, General. Just because Lee surrendered to Grant at Appomattox, doesn't mean the war is over. If you ever hope to see Julia again, we must move quickly."

When Charlie said her name, he remembered how as a boy he had admired her. When he grew older, the attraction was deeper with every passing year. Charlie held her in his mind every moment of his waking hours and dreamed of her at night. It was not just her beauty that spoke to him. She stood apart from other women. She was decisive though gracious, not given to small talk, and in command of every situation. Charlie could hardly remember a time when he was not in love with her. He had been hostage to her milk-white skin, glistening black curls and the intelligence that flashed from her dark eyes for a long, long time.

Fueled by whiskey, General Robert Toombs raised his head and charged down the back steps as though he couldn't wait to get into a fray. He leapt on his large mare unsteadily. The lieutenant bounded down the steps, and mounted his horse which galloped off in pace with the General's Gray Alice.

Love Rises

Through a cracked windowpane on the second floor, Julia Toombs watched her husband and Charlie depart. She stood for a long time after they were out of sight, feeling equal parts of longing and relief. She longed for Charlie and felt relief due to her husband's departure. She reminisced about life as it once was, when Charlie was younger, in and out of their home. There were parties and gaiety, bountiful tables, music and flowers.

Now our spacious houses, Charlie's among them, speak of war and neglect. The neighbors make heroic efforts to maintain their way of life without the necessities to bolster it. Millionaires Row is now Poverty Row, lined with dilapidated mansions. Our outlying plantations are plundered. All we have left is our will to survive.

Julia looked down at the columns that supported her vast home. Our white columns are no longer white; they're a dingy gray. Of course they're gray. This is the triumph that our Rebels who rode off in their sparkling gray uniforms are left with. I'll see these columns white again if it kills me.

Julia remembered standing on the now sagging steps, waving to the General, the columns of their mansion shining behind her. How she had graced her home as one of the great beauties of the South. She wondered if she was still beautiful, or was she as tarnished as her homestead? With her lifestyle demolished and her beauty fading, what did the future hold?

Before the war, the entire state had gossiped about the feud between Jefferson Davis and her husband. The feud was not just political, although they competed for the presidency of the Confederacy. It was also a question of whose wife was the most beautiful: Varina Davis or Julia Toombs. If there had been a statewide vote, most of Georgia's constituency would have voted for dark-eyed, vivacious Julia. Julia knew this, but at forty-one, if she still retained her beauty, she thought all it had gained her was an old, drunken husband and an obsession with a man twenty years younger—a man who doubtless saw her as an older woman. She lifted her skirts and her chin when she turned from the window and went into her bedroom.

She was seated at her dresser when a thunderous knocking sounded at the front door. Thank God Charlie came in time. I'll manage the Yankees, she vowed.

Unhurriedly, Julia pulled her sleeves further onto her shoulders and moved down the stairs. She opened the still shuddering door. "Yes?" she said calmly.

"Is General Robert Toombs in this house?" the young captain asked.

"No. He is not here. He is not in his house."

When the captain moved to enter, Julia said in a

sharp tone, "You may not enter my home."

"I have orders to search the house to make sure the General is not present," the captain said.

"And who, may I ask, issued these orders?"

"Colonel Redman."

"Please return to your installation and tell your Colonel that surely he is a gentleman who can take the word of a southern gentlewoman."

Gruffly, the Captain threatened, "I have leave to burn your house to the ground if you do not cooperate, ma'am."

"Then burn it." Julia turned and started for the stairs. "I'll be in my boudoir, which I don't intend to leave. But first, please do deliver my message to Colonel Redman." Julia closed the door gently. Shaking, she moved up the steps to her bedroom as regally as Marie Antoinette did when she mounted the steps to the guillotine.

***

The fugitives rode in easy silence. The General had known the lieutenant since birth so he chose Charlie to get him safely past Georgia's picket lines and through Alabama to Mobile, where he would board a boat to New Orleans. There, a steamship would sail from the port city, spiriting the General to Cuba and on to London and Paris.

They were headed to Roanoke, one of the General's plantations in Stewart County near the Alabama border. The two planned to approach under cover of night. Despite Lee's surrender, cavalry units were still on the march. Having burned Atlanta and captured Savannah, Union troops planned to pillage and burn their way East. If they could capture a general wanted for treason, it would make tarrying in Confederate territory worthwhile. Every Union soldier detailed to Georgia knew that President Davis met with his cabinet and dissolved the Confederacy in General Toombs' home town. Each was hoping he would be the one to capture General Robert Augustus Toombs, the South's most colorful general.

"I smell smoke from a campfire about a mile away," Charlie warned as he stopped his horse in the near darkness and looked in all directions. "We must detour."

The General reined in and turned toward home. "I must hold Julia just once more," he ordered. Charlie moved his steed to block the General.

"Please. No. General, follow me. We can't go back. You've sworn publicly never to take an oath to the Union. You must know we're in treasonous retreat. I've got to get you into Alabama and out of the country." With each word, Charlie's tone was more desperate.

At the word *treason*, the General spurred his mount in the wrong direction, and roared above the sound of hooves hitting hard ground. "By God, if standing by Georgia is treason, then so be it," he declared for the second time that day. This time, his words were slurred.

To distract him, Charlie pulled another flask from his pocket, and maneuvered his horse beside the General's. From years of practice, he managed to place the flask in the General's grasp while his horse galloped full speed beneath him.

General Toombs, his full mane of ginger-colored hair streaming behind him, shouted, "Damn the Yankees. I will not be captured. I'd rather be killed."

"Then they'll have to kill me, too, General." Subtly, Charlie turned his horse toward their destination in Stewart County. As she was accustomed, the General's horse, Gray Alice, followed Charlie's lead.

***

Julia sat at her dresser, trying to assure herself that the captain had no intention of burning her home; he just wanted to scare her. She turned her mind to Charlie. Who wouldn't love Charlie? His full, almost petulant lips, belied by the ever-present dimple in his cheek and the merriment in his sea blue eyes, were captivating. He was the most alert, focused person she had ever known. The looks he gave her often weakened her knees to the point that she feared she might fall on the soft Persian carpet in the parlor and beg him to join her. But she had responsibilities to fulfill that outweighed her feelings. She had gone about her household duties, telling herself that she must have misinterpreted the side glances at her bosom, her tiny waist, the occasional visible ankle.

Intellectualizing herself into propriety by supposing Charlie's interest was curiosity about women was over. Charlie was a man now. Her resistance was fading like the last stages of a setting sun.

Even though Julia knew the deaths of her three children, one by one, had adversely affected their marriage and escalated the General's drinking, understanding the cause did not alter the effect. And there had always been other women. As difficult as it was to love a drunk womanizer, she loved her husband. Still, Charlie would be back and she would have him to herself. Julia removed the pins and gave her dark hair long, regular strokes with her silver-backed, boar-bristle brush. In the mirror, her rich brown eyes sparkled with anticipation. She was certain that Charlie would see the General safely onto a steamship for Paris and be home before the magnolias lost their blooms.

***

Union patrols were heavy along the Chattahoochee River, and General Toombs' capture was a sought-after prize. Charlie and the General were forced to hide in Georgia's hills for the summer before they could risk crossing into Alabama. By the time they could safely leave their hideout, the lush, ivory magnolia blooms had turned brown, shriveled, and dropped to the ground. There would be a crispness in the air swirling with fallen leaves before Charlie could return home.

***

Mobile, Alabama

By barge, wagon, train, and foot, Charlie delivered the General to Mobile where he was welcomed by the household of Howard Evans, and his sister, Augusta Jane Evans, the well-known southern author. Immediately, she dismissed the servants for the General's safety until such time as his ship, "The Creole," was scheduled to sail for New Orleans. Charlie and the General enjoyed the Evans' hospitality for several weeks. Charlie read constantly. In addition to books from her library, Augusta Jane allowed him access to the manuscript of her forthcoming book, *St. Elmo*. The book's intellectual, capable heroine served only to bring Julia to the forefront of his mind.

While Charlie read, the General flirted with Augusta Jane Evans on endless walks in the garden. Charlie heard them through the open window in his room.

The General said, "It tore my heart out to leave Gray Alice at the river even though she is in good hands with our overseer. She neighed and neighed like a baby crying when Charlie and I took the barge across."

Charlie watched as Augusta Jane moved her body closer and linked her arm in his. Charlie knew she had particularly enjoyed the general's visit since few with his intellect and charm were ever guests in the Evans' home.

"How sad for you," she said with a catch in her voice. "And how sad that because of your beliefs, you must suffer the loneliness of exile." Charlie noticed the woman's moist eyes as the General took her hand and led her to a garden bench.

As the two sat side by side on the bench, Charlie closed the window and calculated the risk level for the journey from Mobile to New Orleans. *It's time to go.*

Through Confederate patriots, the General's passage was already arranged on the *Alabama* from New Orleans to Cuba. From the safety of Cuba, the General would sail to London and on to Paris.

***

Charlie walked General Toombs to the gangplank. Before he moved upward, the General rested a hand on Charlie's shoulder. "Take care of Julia, Charlie. Take care of my wife. Do whatever you must to keep her safe and happy."

"I will," Charlie answered. He stood on the wharf until the *Alabama* set sail. *How long will his exile last? It may be years. It could be forever unless the charges for treason are dropped.* The General gave a half wave, half salute from the deck, a beautiful woman at his elbow. Charlie returned a full salute. *This mission is over. Julia is my mission now.*

Chapter 2
Charlie Returns

Lieutenant Charles Irving moved faster without the General. Also, enough time had passed so there were fewer Union troops to avoid. By train, wagon, and now on foot, he knew he was just a few miles from the river which separated his state from Alabama. Charlie crossed Murder Creek near Evergreen and took a makeshift ferry over the Chattahoochee River to Georgia.

His first stop was Roanoke, the Toombs' plantation. Dusk was falling as he made his way to the slave quarters where smoke spiraled from a chimney. "James! James!" he called. The caramel-colored, powerfully built overseer flew out the door of a cabin and the two men embraced.

"I'm glad you made it through the Yankee lines, Charlie. Is the General safe?"

"On the way to Havana by now. James, I need your fastest horse. I must get home."

"There's the General's horse, Gray Alice. She's more reliable, but not the fastest. I'll give you Charger. He's feisty, but sure-footed and fast."

When James brought Charger from the barn, Charlie leapt on him. With a thankful wave, he was off toward home, toward Washington, Georgia.

Charlie's mind was in a fever. The General's last words to him thundered in his head: "*Take care of Julia, Charlie. Take care of my wife. Do whatever you must to keep her safe and happy.*" How would Julia receive him? Charlie was totally aware that he had been in love with Julia Toombs since puberty. But how did she feel? Dare he hope for intimacy with the most beautiful woman in the South? How could he, a soldier of the Confederacy, betray his general? But the war was over. The General might never return from exile. She would need him for her protection.

The closer he came to his home place, the more Charlie imagined Julia held no interest in him beyond that of any other neighbor. He passed the home of his parents and knew he should look in on his father who was in failing health, but he couldn't wait to see

Julia. He would see his parents after he delivered his message to her. Charlie forced himself to slow his horse to a trot as he moved up the path lined with giant magnolia trees that led to the Toombs' mansion. He tied Charger's reins to the hitching post and ran up the steps, forgetting his weariness.

The young lieutenant rapped on the door with the heavy bronze knocker in the shape of a lion's head. All he heard was a hollow sound from within. Perhaps she wasn't there. He was almost tearful with disappointment as he turned to leave. At that moment the door opened and Julia stood in the waning light. She wore a ruby red velvet dress that set off her shoulders and added depth to her dark eyes.

Charlie stepped over the threshold and stammered, "I, I bring news of the General; he is safe and..." Julia shrugged her shoulders and the red dress fell in a near perfect circle at her feet. She wore no petticoats, no corset, nothing. Charlie was struck speechless. For the first time, he realized what the phrase "heart in your throat" meant.

As Julia mused that there was at least one advantage gained from not having enough to eat, Charlie removed his trousers even faster than Julia's underweight body had slipped out of her dress.

The Lieutenant was not entirely inexperienced with women. When he was younger, a kind slave woman named Tilde, eighteen years older, had patiently showed him what a woman liked, and how to give it to her, introducing him to the signs that announced when a female was ready. Charlie speculated that Julia had been ready for some time. With his first few thrusts, he found he was correct, but he slowed to a gentle rhythm which he knew would give her pleasure.

After the light was gone and the moon had risen to cast an ocean of pale yellow across the stair hall, Julia was the first to speak. "I've been wanting you since you were sixteen years old," she said.

Charlie nodded and rolled off her. "And I, you, my love." He gasped as he realized the brass buttons on his tunic had drawn blood across her breasts. "How can you ever forgive me?" Charlie cried. "I've injured you in my haste to make love to you."

"Forgive?" She reached for her dress, and used it to wipe off the blood. "Let's start over in a different position."

Charlie swept her into his arms, careful of her breasts, and started up the winding staircase to Julia's bedroom. His mind raced. *I have to think of something different before we get there. I can't lay her on her stomach; it will hurt her breasts. On her side? No. Too ordinary. Stand her against the bedpost? No. That might hurt her again.* He entered the high-ceiling room and looked around. *Thank God there's enough moonlight to see.* He knew immediately what to do. Charlie set her on the cherry wood wash stand, spread her legs, and poured the water from the pitcher over her breasts to soothe them. He kissed her and used the remaining wetness that streamed down her belly to spread her lower lips until they were slippery beneath his moving fingers.

"Oh, Charlie, the water's so cold," Julia cried. And then, it was warm.

When Julia finally slept, he went to untether Charger. He fed and watered him and placed him in a stall in the barn

***

At first light, Charlie stoked the stove in the kitchen, heated water, and poured it into the copper tub. He washed himself thoroughly, soaped his beard and shaved, using a razor he found in the cupboard. He dried himself with a dish towel, cleaned the tub, and repeated the heating process. Naked, he went up to the General's room, found a clean white shirt with no collar and a pair of trousers. They were too large, but he put them on and entered Julia's adjoining room. He woke her with a kiss. She stretched lazily and kissed him back. "Ummm," she sighed.

"Good morning, my beauty, your bath is ready." He picked her up, retraced his steps, placed her in the tub, and began to bathe her breasts.

"The damage is not as severe as I thought." He soaped her perfectly rounded orbs twice, sluicing clear water over them.

"No. It's minor. The marks will heal within the week." Gracefully, a slim arm emerged from the water. Her long, tapered fingers held a slippery, green square. "Where did you get this lovely, lovely soap?"

"From the Evans' home in Mobile. There was a giant basketful as a gift for guests. It's olive soap from France." The unspoken thought between them was that the Evans' home had harbored the General.

"I'm glad you brought one home, even though I'm now olive-scented. Do you think you can forage some breakfast? I'm famished."

"What is there?" he asked.

"We still have the cow. There's chicory for coffee, and if you can find a hen's nest, we can share an egg or two."

"Done," said Charlie. He reasoned that a chicken was far easier to sneak up on than a Yankee installation.

***

Charlie heard a cluck, cluck from the woods behind the house and headed for it. Without snapping one twig, he moved toward the hen. When she let out a squawk and a series of cackles that meant she had layed an egg, he lunged. Charlie took a length of string from his pocket. He looked at the string and considered not taking the hen since a laying hen was valuable, but concern for Julia's health overcame him.

He decided he could find another hen and build a chicken coop. Charlie tied the hen's feet and reached for the egg. He had hoped for two, but there was only one.

At the house, he left the hen on the porch and entered the back door with the egg cradled in one hand. He held it out toward Julia. "See what I found. And the hen's on the back porch for Sunday dinner."

Julia rewarded him with a radiant smile. "I never doubted you could find an egg. But I didn't even dream of roasted chicken."

When the coffee was ready and the egg was boiled, Charlie and Julia sat down at the table. "Here, Lovely, take the shirt," he said and wrapped it around her shoulders.

"I may not be able to get through breakfast for looking at your bare chest," she said.

"More likely than if I was looking at yours," he laughed.

"Charlie, we have to be careful, we can't carry on like this all the time. My husband is revered by most of Georgia, and the neighbors are watching. Besides, I feel horribly guilty."

"I feel guilty, too, but the General asked me to look after you; to do whatever it takes to keep you safe and happy," he said.

"Not all day and all night."

"No, but I can come every day, tend your garden,

and see to your needs."

"You know my needs take about three hours at a stretch. How're we going to manage it?"

"We'll manage because we have always loved each other." Charlie looked over at the gray, long-haired cat lying under the stove. "I have a plan," he said. "What's the cat's name?"

Julia smiled. "Drummer Boy."

"How'd he get a name like that?"

"When I'm abed, Drummer Boy loves to sit on my stomach and drum his paws on my breasts. First one and then the other."

"What a clever cat he is. He's just what we need."

Charlie got up from the table, petted Drummer Boy, kissed Julia goodbye, and left for his parents' home.

Chapter 3
Love and Turmoil

Although Charlie's personal slave, Tilde, was freed before the war began, she chose to stay with Charlie and the Irving family whose home stood a short way from the Toombs' mansion.

"Tilde," Charlie confided, "I'm desperately in love. I must see Julia Toombs as much as possible."

"I've suspicioned that since you was twelve," Tilde said.

"It's the nights that are a problem. Julia will feed her cat, Drummer Boy, in the morning and I'll feed him here in the late afternoon. Can you fashion a collar with some sort of pocket or opening so that Julia can send me a message every day and let me know if her evenings are free?"

"Lord, God, Handsome Boy, what if that cat gets hisself killed on the way from the Toombs' house to ours, and somebody reads the message?"

"That's a chance we'll have to take. Can you make a collar, Tilde?"

"Anything for you, Handsome Boy. I believe in true love."

"Do you know how truly I love you, Tilde?"

"I truly do, Handsome Boy." She touched his dark hair and left to get a strong needle and some harness scraps from the slave quarters.

***

Within a few days, Drummer Boy had learned the routine: breakfast at the Toombs' mansion and late afternoon dinner at the Irving home. Julia and Charlie were more than eager to share their meager rations in order to get messages to one another. Drummer Boy was happy to comply. He was getting more food than he had since the war began. The messages were necessarily terse in order to fit into his collar: "visitors 3 days, then come" or "time to plant."

***

As a surprise for Julia, Charlie made the trip one more time to the Toombs' plantation in Stewart County. He retrieved the General's horse, Gray Alice, and led her home.

Knowing it was a perfect excuse to see Julia, Charlie tethered his horse, Young Alice, along with Gray Alice, then ran up the steps to the Toombs' mansion. He rapped on the door. "Mrs. Toombs, Mrs. Toombs," he called just in case someone was in earshot. "I've brought Gray Alice home."

Julia had already heard the hooves of the two horses. She looked out the cracked window pane by the upstairs balcony, and raced down the stairs. She discarded her clothes and appeared at the door wearing absolutely nothing. This time, Charlie was half prepared. "For godsakes, put on some clothes and meet me in the barn," he pled. He hurried the horses to the barn and put them in facing stalls, leaving the stall doors open.

Julia opened the barn door, stepped in, locked it, stepped out of her well-worn brown silk dress and ran to Charlie. He hoisted her onto Gray Alice, then leapt on to the obediently stationary steed from behind, and joined himself to Julia who lay back on Gray Alice's mane as if she was in her own bed.

As Charlie thrust into her with more and more force, Julia dug her thighs and knees into Gray Alice, who still did not move a muscle.

When the lovers were exhausted, Julia said, "I feel like Lady Godiva."

"And I feel really, really glad that I brought Gray Alice home. How do you suppose she knew to remain so still?"

"Charlie, you are impossibly naïve. Don't you know the General compromised every woman who ever flashed a coquettish glance at him? And that probably included some of his soldiers' wives at the encampments."

"I was there and I never suspected anything like that."

"You're not his wife. I suspect he entertained women in Mobile. And then more in New Orleans until his ship sailed. God only knows who boarded with him."

"Maybe," said Charlie, who remembered the woman at the General's elbow as the *Alabama* set sail. He was a little uncomfortable with this news so knowingly delivered from Julia. "Let's go to the house. You're getting cold. We'll warm you by the stove in the kitchen, and then I'll carry you upstairs to bed."

"Why don't you make love to me on every step so I won't need to be warmed by the stove?"

"Done," said Charlie. He helped her down from Gray Alice, and she dressed as quickly as he did. On the way out of the barn, Charlie remarked, "There're twenty-three steps."

***

When they arrived in Julia's bedroom, Drummer Boy was on the bed. Charlie moved to pick him up and Julia said, "Oh, let him stay and warm me, Charlie."

"Warm you? I thought that's what the steps were for."

"I can't get too warm, can I?"

"Absolutely not," said Charlie, and placed Drummer Boy on her stomach.

After a few minutes watching Drummer Boy pound his beloved's breasts, Charlie lifted the big cat off her and set him on the floor. "It's my turn, Drummer Boy." With a great leap, the feline landed on the wash stand, curled himself into the wash basin, and rested his head on the rim to watch.

Charlie rained kisses on Julia's neck and shoulders as he unpinned her hair. "I love you beyond any sacred allegiance I've ever known: to Georgia, to the General, to my home and parents. An endless list. Love rises above all."

"And I feel the same, Charlie. Men think they have a stronger love, but they do not." She breathed deeply, which made her breasts rise as he held her hair and stroked it.

"Do you love me enough to trust me, Julia?"

"Of course."

He kissed both her breasts and suckled each until her nipples were taut. He looked into her eyes.

"There's a trick all soldiers know that keeps them alert when they're standing guard." He sat her up, parted her long hair, tied each half to opposing bed posts and secured them with two of his pocket hand-kerchiefs. Then he spread her legs and began a slow, easy rhythm inside her. As he increased his thrusts, she pulled against her hair, which rushed oxygen to her brain like a drug. Julia screamed, not in pain, but with the pure joy of complete awareness in every part of her being.

They lay in silence for a long time until Charlie spoke. "There's something I have to tell you, Julia. There's trouble along the coast and I have to go. Then there's the constitutional meeting in Milledgeville on the fifteenth. I won't be back until after." He hesitated for a few seconds. "And there might be trouble there, too."

Julia sat up. "Now that the Confederacy is dis-solved, surely the Union understands Georgia has to reorganize and elect Confederate legislators. The war is over. What trouble on the coast?"

"Sherman had so many Negros following his army that he issued Field Order 15, which gave each of them forty acres and a mule so they would disperse. The trouble is, each of the forty acres was confiscated from a plantation owner. The owners want their land back."

"Can't Georgia legislate the return of their properties after the state government is reinstituted?"

"We're going to try. Meanwhile, we have to get the Negros off of their land."

"Charlie! Tell me you're not part of those raider groups."

"Of course not, Julia. I'm a soldier, not a raider. But there are far worse organizations forming that plan to burn and kill. They even intend to conceal their identities. Many of us want no part of that. Some of the younger officers from surrounding counties have gotten together. We call ourselves the Red Persuaders, after your red dress, my love. There'll be no violence."

"And what do you Red Persuaders intend to do? Brandish my red dress and scare the darkies away?"

"No. We'll persuade the Negros to leave the plantations or sign the land back and stay on to work for the plantation owners."

Julia pulled the sheet up over her breasts. "And you think that will be easy?"

"Not always. Some have registered their forty acres in court so there's nothing we can do about that. Some will want to fight, but we won't display weapons and most of the former slaves have none. Others will flee inland."

She ran her forefinger over the hem of the frayed sheet. "And you're going to accomplish all of this before the middle of November? We're so many miles from the coast. The Butler Plantation is there and James told me that since her divorce, Fanny Kemble is hiding out in Major Butler's slave quarters. So she can see her children without Butler's knowledge. I'm sure she'll help you."

Charlie drew her closer. "I'll find her. Distance is no problem, we're young. We'll ride day and night. We'll do what we can and I'll be back right after Milledgeville. It's a possibility, but we don't expect much trouble there."

Julia laid her head on Charlie's shoulder. "Six hundred and fifty thousand dead. You survived, but you want to continue the war. There're still Yankee troops out there. I cannot lose you. Our love won't allow it." She began to weep. "Oh, Charlie, don't leave me. I miss your touch; the only touch I want. I miss your breath on my body. I miss *you*."

He patted her back as he held her. "Just for a little while."

Julia looked at him, her face awash with tears. "But the war is over."

He placed a hand on her cheek and looked into her eyes. "The war will never be over, Julia."

***

Although there were seven members of the Red Persuaders, only two joined Charlie on the trip: Rolly Anderson from Wilkes county and James Battle, educated freedman and overseer at the Toombs' Stewart

County plantation.

The three men made their way through dense forests of pine, oak, and hickory trees often surrounded by holly and climbing vines. Their horses moved at a fast clip through ironweed and other plant impediments, their riders alert to possible Union cavalry.

When they were about halfway to the coast, James shot a rabbit, and they stopped long enough to build a small campfire to cook it. All three of them squatted on the ground, flat-footed as they shared the rabbit around the little ring of fire under a luminous yellow-leaf hickory tree. A twig snapped and Charlie and Rolly froze while James drew his pistol and prepared to shoot. A raccoon scurried up the tree, and they all laughed.

After a relieved moment, Charlie spoke. "James, do you know how well trained Gray Alice is?"

"Course I do, Charlie. I trained her."

Charlie took a bite of the hare. "Doesn't matter what you do on her, she won't move until you tell her."

James rose and rubbed his hands together as though washing them. "She can be a traveling bed, for sure. What you been up to, Charlie?"

Charlie flushed. "Nothing, I just stacked some things on her back without even a rope and she didn't move an inch."

"Hmmm," said the older man.

Shifting the subject, Charlie asked the other two, "How much trouble do you see in front of us?"

"Plenty," said Rolly. When he stood, he was several inches taller than the other men. The plaid tam on his sandy hair advertised his Scottish ancestry. His saddlebags sported a crest, and there was always a faint air of doom about him.

"Not so, Rolly," James said, putting out the fire with a few stamps of his large feet. "I think our timing is right. Some of these new owners may know how to work the land, but they don't know how to get seed or sell or keep books. They may be relieved to see us."

Charlie breathed a prayer, "Lord, I hope so."

"A lot of the forty-acre property is rice land along the coast," James pointed out. "Unless the new owners come from the coastal marshes of Africa, they know nothing about growing rice."

"Let's get to it," said Charlie. "We have an ally in Major Butler's ex-wife at the Butler Plantation. Fanny Kemble is a Brit whose slaves are now freedmen."

"Ex-wife? Anyway, what good to us is an actress?" Rolly asked.

"She never believed in slavery, Rolly," Charlie answered. "She believes in good wages, a share in the crops, and a better life for freed slaves. We'll stop there first. She's hiding out in the slave quarters so she can see her daughters. Since their divorce, Major Butler has custody and he won't allow her to visit them."

"Sounds good to me," Rolly said. "Maybe she'll give us tea."

"Don't make fun of her, Rolly. Fanny Kemble Butler is a woman ahead of her time. She sees no color. She's almost singlehandedly responsible for all five hundred of their freed slaves staying to work the Butler Plantation. The Negros love her. After she left Butler and divorced him, work conditions deteriorated. She plans to reinstitute a better life for the freedmen when she takes over the plantation after Butler dies."

Rolly righted his tam-o'-shanter and gave its little feather a pat. "May the Saints preserve my Scottish mother. How in tarnation does she expect to do that?"

Charlie mounted his horse. "Major Butler is on his last legs with malaria and his daughters will inherit. Mrs. Butler plans to run the plantation after he dies."

Rolly threw a leg over his dappled horse. "Let's see what we can do before women take over all the plantations."

"It's late," said James as he mounted his horse. "Don't forget there's a passel of Yankees between us and the coast. If any one of us hears or sees anything irregular, hold up a hand and we'll all hide."

After a while, they came across a line of tethered Union horses. James held up his hand and motioned for everyone to dismount. When they were past the Union encampment, all three of them let out a long breath.

"I figured their horses were not that close to their camp," James explained. "The Union soldiers wouldn't hear us if we dismounted and walked."

"I've never been so glad that you were right, James," Charlie whispered.

"No point in having an adventure if there's no adventure," Rolly said. "I love a skirmish, but we didn't know the odds. Thanks, James. You can be my ranking officer anytime."

"Mostly luck," James said as he motioned them forward. "And may Lady Luck be with us the rest of the way."

***

The clouds hung low and dark as they crossed the Darien River. Upon arrival at the Butler Plantation, they paused at the sight of it. It was one of the largest plantations in the South, with a white-columned mansion at least two city blocks long. There were lush grounds in front with giant moss-hung trees lining their approach.

"You two take the horses to the slave quarters where they'll be cared for," Charlie said. "My mother knows Major Butler. I'll announce us, although you can be sure the freedmen in the quarters already know we're here and have told him."

Charlie knocked on the door and Pierce Butler, himself, admitted him. Handsome in a charming, rakish way, Butler played the cordial southern host to Charlie as the young lieutenant explained his mission. After he heard Charlie out, Butler said, "Something along those lines has to happen or we will all be penniless and lose our lands. Tell the men to take the horses along to the stables. The slaves will take care of them. Now, let's have a drink, Charlie. How is your lovely mother, Belle?" The older man motioned to a wing chair by the fire. "Tell me, then I'll show you to your guest suites. There are three of you?"

Charlie spoke haltingly. "Uh, one of us is a freed slave."

"Well, he can find a place in the slave quarters. Do I know your colleague?"

"Yes, sir. It's Roland Anderson from Wilkes County."

"Ah yes, I know his relatives well. Unfortunate name in these times. Andersonville will go down in infamy. We treated our slaves better than those soldiers. They deserved more from us, even though they were Union Army."

There was a knock on the door. When Butler rose to answer it, he faltered, and Charlie could see the Captain had been hiding his failing health behind extreme cordiality.

***

In the slave quarters, Fanny Butler was indeed serving tea to freedman James Battle, properly, from her best English porcelain. She served tea as if she was on stage, each motion slow and deliberate. The shack was clean, with a wooden floor and a pump at the sink. The beds were appointed with beautifully designed quilts, and a fire roared in the Jefferson stove. James and Ibo, who inhabited the place, were the only guests for tea.

"Thank you, Mrs. Butler," James said as he looked into her eyes and accepted the delicate cup. He took a sip and turned to Ibo, whose ebony face, in sharp contrast to James' caramel-colored complexion, shone in the firelight. "Please tell me, Ibo, what I should say to the liberated slaves on nearby plantations so that they can have the life you have."

Ibo sat ramrod straight in his cane chair. He cast a grateful look at Fanny, who commanded all the attention without saying a word. "Not all plantations were lucky enough to have a Miss Fanny. She educated us and treated us fairly. Things still look good here, but since she left, we are overworked and often go unpaid. But there's hope. Hope for when Miss Fanny's plan of regular work hours, pay and a share come to pass. That's what I suggest you offer, James. You'll get few refusals. I'll go with you if you like." Ibo stood up.

"But I'll leave you for now," he said. When he stepped out the door, he remembered the silent look of recognition that had taken place between him and Rolly Anderson as they tended the horses. Ibo made a sound between the coo of the dove and hoot of the owl, known to his fellows. It carried through the softness of the night like words over water.

From the steps at the back of the mansion where Rolly Anderson waited, there was an answering call. Eagerly, the Scotsman rose and went into the moonlit night to meet Ibo.

***

The moment that Ibo shut the door, James and Fanny fell on each other like two thirsty people who had found an oasis in the desert. Without a word, James laid her on the bed and they made a surging, passionate union that caused the little bed frame to crack against the wall like a wood cutter's ax, regular and loud.

When they were finished, Fanny said, "I'm sorry I couldn't say anything earlier, my dearest. I was too stunned to see you."

"You know I come to you whenever possible, but now that we have Lily, I must be more vigilant. Even though our marriage is recorded, it's still against the law. Discovery would mean a slow and painful death for us all, my dear."

"I know. I know. I wish I could wave a wand and

place the three of us fifty years in the future."

James covered Fanny's naked body with the quilt. "Or a hundred years."

Fanny placed her cheek next to his. "The next best thing would be for all of us to sail for England, my darling. While our union might not be entirely acceptable, we wouldn't be killed."

James clasped her quilt-clad body in his strong arms. "We can't. Not yet. Maybe not ever. I might get out of the country with you as your servant, but Lily would never be allowed as our daughter."

Fanny shed the quilt, pulled on her dress, and buttoned it as she moved toward the fire. "Oh, let's quit dreaming of the future and find our joy in this moment, in our child, and in our memories. Tell me how we met. Tell me about the night we were married. Tell me of Lily. Even the smallest detail is food for my soul. I want to hear it all, from the beginning."

James came up behind her, took her by the shoulders and turned her to face him. The firelight played over their faces and their eyes met as only two souls who have become one can. James began in a deep tone that harked back to a circle of his people in Africa listening to stories around an open fire.

"Carlton Winfrey was among a group of young Methodist ministers who came south just before the war started. They were just out of seminary and full of high ideals. Those young men came here to talk

Southerners out of the abhorrent practice of slavery. But they reckoned without the beautiful women and mint juleps on verandas taken with convivial conversation. There was a softness to life, yet also a resistance to the death against anyone who challenged their way of life. Theirs was a life undergirded and maintained by slavery.

"Everyone was polite to those ministers, especially to Carlton Winfrey who had the manners and good looks to move in southern society easily. He married a southern belle from a plantation near Roanoke. Carlton always treated me as a man, not as a slave, as an equal intellect, not a lowly piece of humanity to be sold or traded. We played chess and talked into the night, many times in my little cabin. He could never understand my allegiance to the Toombs family, as you cannot. Yes. I was born a slave, but I obtained my freedom by hard work and a close bond with each member of the Toombs family.

"When the war broke out, Carlton stayed home and preached and I continued to work the land as best I could. When you were writing your book about slavery and you came to Roanoke, neither of us could believe that we fell in love. Our attraction was so powerful that we could almost hear it. You knocked on my door and I came out to talk. You could barely ask questions and I was so stunned by our instant connection that I could barely answer. But what could we do? How could love survive in Georgia be-tween a Negro man and a white, married, foreign woman? Eventually, you were able to divorce Butler. When Lily was on the way, I turned to Carlton. I knew he could make the necessary arrangements even though our union was illegal.

It was after midnight when you and I arrived at that tiny church in Crawford. Carlton chose Taliaferro County because it was the smallest county made of pieces from other counties and entirely overlooked by most Georgians. In the dead of night, in the middle of a rare snowfall, I became the luckiest man in the world when you became my wife, Fanny Kemble But-ler Battle." James bent down and gave her a slow, lin-gering kiss.

She looked into his eyes and stepped back. "Now, tell me about Lily," she said. "When do you think we'll be able to make it known that Lily is our daughter? I want the world to know I'm alive and I'm her mother. I yearn to have her between us, our arms around her."

"Again, my love, the answer is, not now, maybe never. I must remind you, you were the one who said, 'Backstage is no place for a baby; Lily must have one constant parent with her at all times,' and that parent is constrained by his color." James kissed Fanny again with a passion that shut out the world around them.

Chapter 4
The Ladies of the Row

Although there were good distances between their houses, the families who inhabited them called their homes, "The Row." All of the houses were white-columned, with several stories and steep steps that led up to wide verandas. "The Row" houses, initially known as Millionaires Row, served as in-town residences, although some of the owners also had plantations fronted by stately homes. Other owners tired of the distance from town and moved their plantation houses to "The Row."

Three of the ladies of "The Row" met each Tuesday for tea. Sometimes there were a few tea leaves. In the summer there were tomato sandwiches if anyone had flour for bread, and in the winter, often there was only boiling water which they all pretended was tea, taken with a few pecans from local trees.

Always in attendance were: Dattie Tucker who rarely said a word, Charlie's mother, Belle Irving, who educated her slaves and was a bit suspect by the other two, and finally, Euphemia Foscue, the town busybody, hatchet-faced and thin lipped. Euphemia was the oldest and therefore felt an obligation to preside over tea in her home.

Julia Toombs was always invited, but rarely accepted. She was much younger than the others and was a well-known hostess in the nation's capital when the General had served in Congress as senator. These two facts set her aside from the others who lived on "The Row."

While Julia liked Charlie's mother, Belle, immensely, her dislike for Euphemia Foscue generally outweighed her fondness for Belle Irving. Today, Julia accepted with hope of learning if the other three were suspicious of Charlie's continual presence at her home.

The tea table was set with Euphemia's finest, most ornate sterling tea service. Some of the Haviland teacups were cracked but still beautifully delicate with small pink flowers and trailing leaves.

The ritual began. "Thank God those vile Yankees

didn't get your tea set or your china, Euphemia," Dattie Tucker said.

Euphemia sniffed. "Only because I buried it."

"And because Sherman didn't feel it necessary to detour here," Belle Irving said.

Euphemia Foscue ignored the comment. "Before Julia arrives, I want to know what you think about Drummer Boy roaming from the Toombs' mansion to your house every day, Belle."

Before Belle could answer, uncharacteristically, Dattie Tucker spoke. "I think cats are a lot smarter..."

With a slight motion of her hand, Euphemia cut her off, and Dattie sank deeper into the down cushions at the back of her chair, a movement which caused the tight little ringlets atop Dattie's head to settle also.

"Belle, please tell me what that cat expects at your house every day," the hostess inquired.

"Dinner, my dear," Belle Irving said drily. There was a knock on the door and since Euphemia was ensconced behind the tea table, Belle went to answer it. "Julia, how delightful of you to join us. I've been meaning to call. I miss Charlie and I know you do, too."

"More than I can say, Mrs. Irving," Julia replied as she entered Euphemia Foscue's parlor, resplendent in a low cut, light green sateen. She nodded to Dattie Tucker, and turned to Euphemia. "It's so kind of you to continue to have us for tea in these hard times, Mrs. Foscue. I've brought chicken sandwiches."

Euphemia's chin came up. Insulted, but eager to have real chicken tea sandwiches to serve her guests, she took the artfully arranged offering and replied, "Please be seated, Julia. We were just discussing your cat."

Julia sat down and leaned toward Euphemia. "With our Charlie and other Wilkes County heroes fighting for plantation owners' rights on the coast, you were talking about Drummer Boy? Whatever for?"

Euphemia straightened her spine and poured a cup of tea for Julia. "We just wondered what he was up to."

Julia took the watery tea and smiled. "If you mean Drummer Boy, he's up to what the rest of us are up to, Mrs. Foscue, finding food. Would you please pass me a chicken sandwich? And I would love it if you would place one of your pecan halves on top."

Chapter 5
Charlie Returns from the Coast and Milledgeville

Charlie arrived in Washington at dusk. Without trying to find Drummer Boy, he rode Young Alice down the broad lane to the hitching post in front of the Toombs' mansion. He took the front steps two at a time. Forgetting to call out "Mrs. Toombs," in case anyone was in earshot, he shouted, "Julia! Julia!" He turned the ornate metal doorknob in the shape of a T, found it open and continued to call as he raced up the circular stairs, his boots pounding out his haste.

He opened her bedroom door to see Julia turn

from her dressing table, brush in hand. "Thank God, you're all right."

Charlie was too anxious to sweep her into his arms and lay her on the bed. He placed her full length on the white marble top of her dresser.

Julia reached her arms toward him. "Oh, Charlie. I've missed you so."

Still standing, he entered her and after a few thrusts, pulled her upright so that her heels were on the dresser's edge. Clasping her back, he smothered her with kisses on her face, neck, and finally her shoulders. He pulled her dress down around her waist and kissed her breasts, never losing his rhythm.

Silently, Drummer Boy padded into the room and jumped into the wash basin. He did not have to watch long. He was a little puzzled when Julia dropped the brush she held.

"Drummer Boy is making a ritual of this," Charlie observed as he lifted Julia off the dresser. "Does his presence bother you?"

"Not at all. I rather like it. And he seems to enjoy watching us. Let's rid ourselves of this dress and start over somewhere else."

"I bow to you; I'm grateful for your promptings," Charlie said formally with a grin. He pulled her dress to the floor and carried her to the double armoire. A slab of white marble attached the two side closets of the armoire, which left just enough width for Julia's hips with Charlie's arms beside them.

Charlie adjusted the mirrored doors so that the two of them could watch themselves as he stood naked in front of Julia. With a hand on each cheek of her derriere, he pulled her toward him.

Drummer Boy raised his head to look at this new action reflected in triplicate. He watched in wonder for a while and then felt called upon to jump down, grasp the brush handle in his jaws, leap on the bed and wait.

When they finished making love, Julia said, "Look Charlie. I think Drummer Boy wants us to brush him."

"No. I'm sure he wants me to brush you." He carried Julia with her legs around his waist to the bed and placed her head against the pillows. Charlie brushed the curly mass between her thighs, and said, "What a gorgeous box you have."

Julia sat up. "What? What box?"

"I'm sorry, my love. It's a crude term that soldiers use. I didn't mean to disrespect you. It's that yours is covered in such soft beauty." He laid his hand on the nest of curly hair that he had just brushed.

Julia laughed. "I think it's humorous," she said. "And what do the soldiers call this?" she asked, pulling on Charlie's erection.

"I'm not telling you that," he said, brushing Drummer Boy off the bed. "But I can show you."

Drummer Boy returned to the wash basin. When Charlie began to brush the long hair on Julia's head, Drummer Boy leapt up and stationed himself on Julia's stomach.

***

"One of these days, Drummer Boy is going to scratch your breasts," Charlie said as he lay beside Julia.

"I'll take that chance. So far, you are the only one who's damaged them."

"*Touché*," Charlie said. "Do you want to hear about the plantations on the coast and what we did at Milledgeville?"

"Of course. I can't stay in this heaven within me all the time. I was worried sick the whole time you were away. Your absence places me in a far and distant land. You can't imagine how terrible it is to roam these empty rooms and watch for you at the windows with only Drummer Boy for company."

Charlie turned toward her. "Even while we were skirting the Yankees, I was thinking of you every moment," he said as he gathered her closer. "We were very successful along the coast. Most of the original owners have reclaimed their land. James was right. Many of the Negros who have forty acres and a mule have nothing else, and we were able to work out deals very easily."

Julia propped herself up on one elbow. "How successful was the constitutional convention?"

"Very successful. We elected Governor Jenkins and the members of the legislature are nearly all Ex-Confederates. Other than repealing secession, repudiating Confederate debt and abolishing slavery, nothing has changed in Georgia law."

Julia raised herself on one elbow. "You act as though that's nothing. It's quite a lot. What will happen to Georgia's Negros? What will happen to our Negros?"

"Times are hard for all of us, particularly the Negros. But Georgia stands alone as the only southern state that did not adopt a harsh Black Code. I take a little credit for that."

"The Negros will have the same rights we do?"

Charlie leaned over and kissed her. "Most of our rights. They can marry each other and sue and own property. They cannot serve on juries or enter into interracial marriages."

Julia arranged herself on Charlie again. "I can't imagine any Negro would want to marry a white person."

Charlie put his arms around her. "Are you forgetting James Battle? We don't have to ask if Lily's mother was white. Just look at Lily. Who knows what will happen in the future?"

Julia gave a contented sigh and settled herself more comfortably on Charlie. "James brought Lillian over to me last week. I rocked and sang to her by the fireside for a long time. She's such a beautiful child."

Charlie noted the yearning in Julia's eyes and changed the subject. "Have you heard anything from the General?"

Julia stretched full length against Charlie which meant from her head on his shoulder, she reached just below his knees. She raised her head to look at him. "Yes. He's in Havana. London and Paris will follow."

Charlie positioned himself beneath her. "I wonder how long we have until he returns? Everyone in Milledgeville was asking after him. He was almost as big a topic as what happened to the gold that was in the Confederate treasury."

Julia rolled off Charlie and sat up. "Gold? I thought it was all worthless Confederate paper money."

"A lot of it was gold and silver from Virginia banks. It came by train from Richmond to North Carolina and was shunted back and forth from the Carolinas to here in Washington in order to circumvent the Yankees."

"By wagon?" Julia asked.

"Yes. The gold was transported so many times, no one seems to know quite where it disappeared or where it is. Rumors abound that it's buried right here in Wilkes County."

Julia fell back against the pillows. "We could certainly use that gold."

***

It was time. Drummer Boy stole out from under the steps at the Toombs' mansion and headed for Dattie Tucker's house. He and Dattie had something in common: they both liked to dig. Late at night when the moon was full, the two of them headed for the forest.

The giant gray cat took up his post on Dattie's front porch. He understood the importance of their mission so he was prepared to wait.

Soon, Dattie opened the door carefully. She carried a small shovel. When she slid the handle of a spade under Drummer Boy's collar, he stepped proudly down the steps with the spade on his back, careful not to let it slide. Dattie in her long black dress and Drummer Boy with his tail up, moved into the vastness of the silvery night like two voyagers to another world.

When Dattie found a suitable place, she loosened the soil with the spade, put her foot on the shovel, and dug with remarkably powerful scoops at the earth. Drummer Boy joined her. For a cat, he, too, made good progress.

"Dig, Drummer Boy, dig," Dattie said. "When we find the gold, I'll get you some catnip and a velvet pillow to sleep on." She leaned down and stroked his coat, then pulled her shawl tight around her and addressed the moon. "As for me, I want a fur coat with a hood to keep off the damp, and a gold carriage with four white horses."

Drummer Boy took a break and wound himself around Dattie's skirts, then continued to dig even though he felt another unsuccessful night was in store for them. The feline remembered with nocturnal pleasure the time he unearthed a spoon made of silver coin. He sniffed with anticipation at the thought of catnip that would be his when they found the gold.

Again tonight their digging proved unfruitful, but Dattie dreamed on of uncovering the lost gold of the Confederacy, and she and Drummer Boy continued to set out for the forest when the moon was full.

Chapter 6
The Unexpected

Charlie arrived early to work in Julia's garden although there was little to do. He used the hoe on a few weeds. When he searched for potatoes that he had missed harvesting, Drummer Boy joined him in digging.

Shortly, Julia came out to collect the potatoes. She put them in a basket over her arm and said, "Christmas will be here soon. Let's go into the woods and gather some holly. I'll make garlands to run up the banister and across the mantelpiece."

Charlie drew out his pocket knife and said, "Wonderful idea."

The three of them proceeded into the woods where Charlie cut holly and placed it in Julia's basket, throwing longer pieces over his shoulder.

"Even if we don't catch a wild turkey, we can be festive," Julia said, breaking off a sprig of the shiny leaf with a few red berries attached. She placed the sprig under Drummer Boy's collar and said gleefully, "I'm cold. Let's race back to the fire."

The three of them ran, Charlie impeded by the holly on his shoulder, and Julia encumbered by her basket. Drummer Boy was seated on the porch in front of the back door to the kitchen when Charlie and Julia arrived, laughing. Charlie dropped his load of holly and took Julia's basket. He swept her into his arms and kicked open the kitchen door. When they entered the warmth of the kitchen, Charlie lifted her skirt, and placed her in one of the rockers flanking the fireside.

Drummer Boy found his place underneath the big stove, and Charlie unbuttoned his trousers and joined Julia. Drummer Boy noticed that the rocker seemed to go back and forth of its own accord. He thought people and sometimes the things around them were strange, although he reminded himself how much he liked the cool wash basin against his fur.

After they were warm and glowing, Julia said, "Do you like to rock, Charlie?"

"I love it." He motioned to the identical rocker on the far side of the hearth. "We could christen the other rocker right now if you wish."

Julia put her arms around his neck and looked into Charlie's eyes. "Speaking of christenings, I have something to tell you."

Chapter 7
Plot to Capture Drummer Boy

Euphemia Foscue was on watch for Drummer Boy. She thought there was something peculiar about his feeding arrangement, and she meant to find out what lay behind the giant cat's irregular behavior. She wanted to know what would happen if she kept the cat in her house for a few days.

Finally, she gave up striding back and forth behind her windows. Even though it was cool and the sun was setting, she moved on to the porch rocker, taking with her a straw laundry basket and her knitting. In order to lure him, she also brought chicken from the remaining tea party sandwich, put it on a cracked china saucer and set it in front of the rocker. She made these elaborate preparations in spite of the fact that she thought she might have missed Drummer Boy. If Euphemia had paid closer attention, she would know that Drummer Boy made his trips from the Toombs' mansion to the Irving house at the same time every day except on the days that were followed by a full moon. On these days he traveled later so he would not have so long to wait on Dattie Tucker's porch for their nighttime excursion.

It was almost dark when Drummer Boy moved into view at a stealthy stroll. When Euphemia spied him she called, "Here, kitty. Here, kitty, kitty." She picked up the saucer so he could see and smell the chicken.

Drummer Boy evaluated the offering. He weighed the woman's ignorant, "Kitty, kitty," call to a full grown cat against the fact that it did seem to be real chicken. He knew he would receive dinner at the Irving's but it was rarely chicken. He decided to give the chicken a try even though he had picked up a dislike for Euphemia Foscue from his beloved Julia.

Cautiously, he ascended the steps and waited for Euphemia to set the saucer down. Did this woman who reeked of onions and tried to cover it with lavender talcum powder think he would even approach the saucer if she held it?

Finally, Euphemia set the saucer down and re-seated herself in the rocker. When Drummer Boy started eating, she grabbed the laundry basket and slapped it around cat and saucer. "Got you!" Euphemia declared.

What a stupid, stupid, mean woman, Drummer Boy thought. Euphemia pushed the basket with her foot toward the front door and Drummer Boy moved along with it until he finished the chicken. When Euphemia reached for her front doorknob, Drummer Boy gave the laundry basket a shove with his body, followed by a swipe with his powerful tail and sent it sailing. He raced around the corner of the porch and down the back steps. Euphemia tripped over the saucer, righted herself, and pursued him.

Drummer Boy headed for Dattie Tucker's at a furious pace. Euphemia stopped only to pick up a rake leaning against her house as she followed. Drummer Boy made it under the steps at Dattie's house well ahead of Euphemia. When she arrived, Euphemia poked the handle of the rake under the stairs in order to rout him.

Dattie appeared on the steps shouting "Hear! Hear! What are you after under my steps, Euphemia?"

"Oh, just a raccoon that I was chasing away from my trash heap."

For once, Dattie stood up for herself. "All this way, Euphemia? I shouldn't think there's enough edible refuse on the whole Row to attract a raccoon." Remembering her manners, Dattie added, "Perhaps you would like to come in?"

"No thank you, Dattie, I'll be getting along home. I'll see you at tea on Tuesday."

When Euphemia left, Dattie, who was no fool, called softly under the steps, "Drummer Boy, is that you?"

Feeling safe, Drummer Boy emerged and the two went into Dattie's house where she led him into the kitchen. "I'll give you a little tidbit, Drummer Boy. But you know Charlie expects you for dinner."

Drummer Boy looked up at her. "Meow," he said, always happy to forage whatever extras he could on his appointed rounds.

Chapter 8
Julia Joins the General in Paris

Julia and Charlie dressed, went downstairs, and seated themselves in the parlor. Julia sat on Charlie's lap with her arms around his neck. She looked into his eyes. wondering if their child would look at the world though Charlie's shade of blue.

"I'm so glad you're pleased, my love," Julia said.

"A part of you and a part of me is going to join us as a whole new person. Who wouldn't be pleased?" He paused a moment. "Of course, there are complications. A divorce. And the General may challenge me to a duel or shoot me on sight."

Julia laughed. "You don't know the General nearly as well as I do. There's no need for a divorce or a duel. He can hardly complain about what we've been doing since he's been womanizing from the first days of our marriage."

"But I want you for my own. And there's the child."

"The three, or rather the four of us, will work it out. I'll cable him today. I must go to Paris immediately to tell him."

"And I must go with you. I can't let you travel alone in your condition, much less let you face the General alone."

"How do I make you understand, Charlie? There will be no 'facing the General'; he adores me. Whatever woman he's entangled with, he will drop when I arrive in Paris. I always come first with him. And whatever state I am in, he will accept. He loves me."

"I love you more. I cannot share you with another. What kind of man would I be?"

"You're being melodramatic, Charlie. You've already shared me with him, and we'll share our child with him. It's simple, Charlie."

"Simple? Simple? How can you use that word? You're suggesting the most complicated arrangement of all time to play out in front of the whole populace of Washington, Georgia. And how do you know General Toombs will go along with such a plan?"

Julia slid off Charlie's lap to a standing position. "Because he's my husband and I am completely sure of his reaction."

Near tears, Charlie said, "How can I let you go? I'll think of you every hour." He paused a moment to keep his emotions in check. "Thank God for memories. But they become cold and lifeless when I compare them to your presence."

She took his hand. "Let's rock by the warmth of the fire. I want you to think of us there every hour while I'm gone. I'll try to be back before Christmas. If not, I've left a gift and a letter for you. Anyone can read the letter and see a friendly thank you. Only you, my love, will recognize our language of passion, invisible to others."

***

When Julia arrived in Paris, she was helped from her carriage and given over to the hotel employee who greeted her as an expected guest. "The Grande Hotel is at your service in any regard, Mrs. Toombs. You have only to ask."

"First I wish to see my husband."

"Of course," the man replied. "I will escort you, and your luggage will be waiting in your suite with your husband. I am sure you will find the view of the new opera house most impressive. Our concierge will secure tickets if you wish."

"Perhaps later," Julia replied as she was swept

through the lavish lobby which was filled with huge plants. Lounge chairs in intimate arrangements were secreted behind the greenery, and the scent of freesias permeated the air.

The lift took them to the top floor where the General waited. After a soft knock, Julia's escort departed. The General threw open the door and placed his powerful arms around her as he drew her into the room. He held her as though she was his lifeline, his connection to a life now lost to him.

"My darling, darling Julia. To have you and Paris together at last." He kissed her, then held her at arm's length to look at her. "Beautiful as ever."

"It is good to see you looking well, too, my dear. I feared your asthma would be worse in this city."

"Not here. Baron Haussmann has redesigned Paris with fifteen hundred gaslights, aqueducts to carry fresh water, and wide, tree-lined avenues. There are parks and gardens, a beautiful opera house, and a new racetrack called Longchamp. There's even ice skating under Napoleon's Second Empire. We shall do it all."

"I must forego the ice skating," she said, looking at him knowingly.

Instantly, the General knew that refusing a new challenge was unlike Julia, and he thought he knew why. He drew himself to his full height and demanded, "Julia, are you...?"

She looked at him evenly. "Yes. Yes I am."

The General raised a fist. "Who is he? I shall kill him."

"Who, but Charlie? And you shall not kill him. He risked his life for you."

The General strode back and forth, fuming. "How could you, Julia? How could you do this to me?"

"The same way you do it to me. Only their mothers know how many children you have fathered."

At this remark, the General calmed. "True, my love. But the worst of this is what it will do to your reputation."

"No one need know. I'm here and when I return home and give birth to Lucy, we will rear her as our own with Charlie's daily presence."

"How do you know it's a girl?"

"The same way I know you will return soon, and Lucy will be the joy of your old age and keep us abreast of the new century to come."

"You are a remarkable woman, Julia. Too remarkable. But I see no other way to handle this terrible situation."

Julia placed a hand on each of his shoulders and looked into his eyes. "Not one more negative word," Julia said. "Now, let's see Paris."

The General took her in his arms. "First stop will be the House of Worth. We're invited to the Imperial Ball at the Tuileries. You shall have a new gown to rival Empress Eugenie's."

"Bob, we cannot possibly afford such extrava-
gance."

"Yes, my dear, we can. I hadn't wanted to tell you,
but I've sold Roanoke."

Julia paled. "Sold Roanoke! Even though we still
have Greenway and Roanoke's deteriorated, that
plantation's our principal source of income. And
without asking me, how could you sell?"

"Exile is expensive. Paris is expensive. I figure I'm
eating about an acre of Roanoke a day here in the
City of Light."

"Does James know? What will the sale do to him?"

"Yes, he knows. And it will mean no change for him
if the buyer is even half intelligent. James Battle is the
best overseer in Georgia."

Julia's face reddened. "You think this will happen
for James, but you don't know. Lillian is just a baby.
Her mother died in childbirth and James has her
care. That man has given his whole life to Roanoke. Is
dismissal to be his reward?"

The General put his palms out in entreaty. "What
am I to do, Julia? I have living expenses, and I'll be arrested for treason if I go home. But as you indicated,
perhaps the Yankee hounds will cease yapping at my
heels soon, and I can return to you."

***

The General helped Julia into the carriage and said to

the driver, "The House of Worth, number seven, *Rue de la Paix.*" The General stepped into the carriage, seated himself beside Julia and rapped on the ceiling. The driver flicked his horses and they were off down the broad boulevard.

When they arrived, a man in livery helped them out of the carriage and into the splendid surroundings at the House of Worth. Three live mannequins, one blonde, one auburn-haired, and one brunette stood on pedestals around the room in front of mirrored walls. Life size portraits, which included Empress Josephine and Empress Eugenie, separated the mannequins.

Julia nudged her husband and whispered, "We're a long way from Washington, Georgia."

He leaned over and stage-whispered to her. "But, my dear, not one of the mannequins equals your beauty."

At that moment, Charles Frederick Worth greeted them. "Mrs. Toombs, General," he said with a slight bow born of his dealings with kings and queens, emperors and empresses. "It is my pleasure to have the opportunity to provide a setting for such beauty," he said, nodding at Julia. "Mrs. Toombs, if you and the General will be seated on the Empire sofa, I will show you materials for your selection and have Madame Henri take your measurements."

As Julia sank into the down-backed sofa, she

looked around the room. Pier mirrors were every-where and much of the furniture was lacquered in gold. Her eyes fastened on the blonde mannequin in the long gold gown strewn with fabric roses. Accus-tomed to beautiful surroundings, Julia was not the least bit overwhelmed. She joined in as if she were the main character in a play and Mr. Worth her sup-porting actor. Julia's eyes lit with mischief. What fun, she thought.

Worth showed her fabric after fabric, solid color silks in jewel tones, velvets, jacquards. Many of the fabrics were so heavily embroidered that it was diffi-cult to see the material.

Julia viewed each with a look neither of approval nor disapproval. *What a great game*, she mused with-out showing her feelings.

When Worth had exhausted his goods, Julia laid her arm across her abdomen. "Mr. Worth, is it possi-ble to, to…" Here she feigned a mix of coquettishness and embarrassment, "to allow for expansion?"

At the same time the General reprimanded her with "Julia!" Mr. Worth said, "I understand. We have a fabric which has an abundance of give to it. Hard to work with but very effective."

As Worth left to get the sample, she called to him, "In gold, I think."

***

After they were in the closed carriage Julia said, "Bob,

you didn't even ask the cost."

"Cost doesn't matter. What matters, is that with our entrance, every male guest at the ball will fall silent and focus on you."

Julia laid her head on his shoulder as the strong winter light shone through the little back window of the well-appointed carriage. She thought about what he said, raised her head and sat up straight. "General Robert Augustus Toombs, I do wish you would stop regarding me as an ornament you flaunt to impress others."

***

On the evening of the ball, Julia dressed carefully in her new, golden Worth gown. She brought none of her remaining jewelry with her and needed none. Her bosom and her almost bare shoulders emerged from the gown as works of art. They were crowned by her dark eyes and luxurious hair set in long curls with a nest of smaller ones atop her head.

The General stared in awe as she came into their sitting room. "You have the look of a goddess. You rival the Venus de Milo who needed no jewels to set her off. Perhaps a gold fan to complete your look. I purchased it yesterday at one of the nearby shops."

With an imperious gesture, Julia took the fan, snapped it open, laughed and looked over it at her husband.

"Perhaps the fan is too much," he said, viewing her

liquid, brown eyes above the golden lace of the fan.

"I think not, I do not wish you to return such a lovely present. Let's go."

***

When they were seated in the hotel's carriage, the General rapped on the ceiling. "The Tuileries Palace," he said, completely unnecessarily as they joined the late night snarl of carriages headed toward the royal event.

They arrived in front of the long, winged palace overset with a large dome, and were escorted through reception to the landing above the ornate, paneled ball room hung with mirrors and tapestries.

"I've never seen so many chandeliers and gilt in one place before," Julia whispered to the General as they waited to be announced.

As each name was called out, the crowd of guests below turned and nodded perfunctorily.

When the General and his beautiful wife were announced, the crowd turned, the women gave a nod, and the men simply stared and kept on staring until Julia snapped her fan open to indicate *Enough*. Unexpectedly, the orchestra accompanied their descent to the ballroom floor with a lively rendition of "Dixie."

"Even the orchestra adores you. Before you leave Paris, my love, it is my duty to commission Tissot to paint your portrait as you are tonight."

***

James Tissot, an anglicized Frenchman, greeted Julia with kisses on both her cheeks. As they entered his sunlit studio strewn with easels and heavy with the scent of wet paint, he said, "Please be seated. First, we must talk. Before I begin your portrait, I must know what you want and feel in addition to what I want of you."

Julia moved back in her chair, backbone straight, thoroughly aware that she faced a formidable painter with an enviable reputation. "I know exactly what I want. I want my portrait to be of a woman in love, seated in a rocker with a sprig of holly in her hand and a large, gray Persian cat on her lap."

Tissot raised his heavy brows in surprise. "Ah, Americans, even more decisive than the English. Such a joy. But you must let me be in charge of your hands. One must rest upon the other, the fingers separated, with a sprig of holly beneath as if you had just captured it."

"Done," Julia said. "I like you, Monsieur Tissot." She looked at his delicate hands and bright eyes, wondering if his talent came without thought from mind to hand or if he had to concentrate. "I like you so much that I'm going to make you an offer. I shall pose for another, secret portrait with only the holly, if you wish."

The master painter was overcome. With tears in his eyes, he said, "Do you mean nude, my dear?"

"Yes. With only the holly."

"I shall paint you as Titian and Rubens and Veláz-quez before me, with worshipful reverence for your beauty, while maintaining my highest degree of pro-fessionalism."

"I am confident of that. And can you arrange for both portraits to accompany me home when I set sail on the *Alabama*, while my husband rests assured that there is only one very expensive portrait?"

"The Frenchman in me yields completely. Only the two of us will know." He paused a moment. "And per-haps a third?"

"Yes. A gift for my Charlie," she smiled. "But you must conceal my face. I leave it for you to disguise the significance of the holly."

***

On her fifth and last sitting with Tissot, Julia admired the almost finished portrait displaying her beauty in the Worth gown. She paused in thought and then said to the artist, "The cat on my lap bears a remarkable likeness to Drummer Boy. The shine in my eyes is un-mistakably that of a woman in love. The curved ma-hogany rocker gleams, my hands rest on the cat's back, and holly peeps up out of the gray fur as if it grows there. The General will be pleased. So pleased you can double the price to cover the cost of the nude portrait. Isn't it time for us to begin?"

"Yes. Yes. I have it all worked out, if you will permit

me. My father was a draper and my mother a milliner. I know my fabrics and my hats."

"I'm sure you do," Julia replied. "But a hat on a nude?"

"A hat on a nude who must be disguised. Please trust me."

Julia moved behind a gilt screen decorated with water lilies and began to undress. "I do trust you," she called. "Bring on the hat."

When Julia emerged with only the sprig of holly she had garnered from her hotel, Tissot didn't give her nudity a second glance. "Please lie on the chaise and cross your ankles," he directed. When Julia obeyed, he placed a cartwheel hat made of gray horsehair on her head and tilted it to cover three quarters of her face. Then he arranged the dark red velvet fabric around her, folded her hands and placed the holly under the hat's black ribbon that curved around the crown. The artist stood back to admire his composition. "Do you feel red is a good color for the drape?" he asked.

She parted her thighs a little in order to rest more comfortably before she answered him. "Red is a perfect color, and velvet is an intuitive choice for the fabric."

Tissot picked up a brush and dipped into his palette. Wielding the camel's hair as an instrument of love, he invaded the canvas with sure strokes. "I need only do a study from your live pose, Madame. Your body is burned into my memory."

***

Julia arrived in her suite at The Grande with high color, which her husband noticed immediately. "Come lie with me," he said, leading her to the big, canopied bed. The General tossed a down pillow under her hips and disrobed.

Unconsciously, Julia crossed her ankles, then uncrossed them and opened her thighs with one leg off the edge of the mattress and the other encompassing the General's back as they were accustomed. "Charge!" shouted the General.

Chapter 9
Home for Christmas

Julia boarded the *Alabama* with relief at leaving Paris and the General behind. The General was drinking even more since leisure was forced upon him, and while his devotion to her was unchanged, his actions were edging toward the buffoon. She could hardly wait to see Charlie come into view on the dock when she reached Mobile. Her gift for him was secured in the ship's hold along with her sedate portrait which would hang above the mantelpiece in the Toombs' mansion.

***

Julia sat on a deck chair encompassed by fog and

wrapped in a blanket to ward off the winter chill.

The woman next to her, similarly wrapped, remarked, "Fanny Kemble, the famous actress, is joining us when we stop at Liverpool, I hear."

By her accent, Julia recognized the woman as a fellow American. "How very delightful. She is well known in Georgia. How did you come by this knowledge?"

The voluptuous woman leaned toward Julia. "I am what the Captain kindly calls 'the ship's hostess,'" she said. "So I'm privy to the secrets of the pillow, or the alcove, as some say. My name is Selena."

"Oh," Julia said, slightly taken aback. "I am happy to know you, Selena, I am Julia DuBose Toombs, of Washington, Georgia." Julia thought the mention of her French maiden name might serve to put the woman at ease.

"I do so yearn for female company. Most women refuse to speak to me, Mrs. Toombs. I'm Selena Wainwright, the last name chosen randomly to deny my Appalachian birth."

Julia cemented their new friendship with laughter and the two began an intimate chat about men, birthrights, and the places women were forced into by society. Julia concluded, "Men are often like children, easily swayed by women. In society, but for our place of birth, I could be the ship's hostess and you could be the first lady of Washington, Georgia." At this remark, Selena smiled.

***

When Fanny Kemble Butler boarded the ship, she caused quite a stir. Her roles on the English and American stage had brought her fame and her published writings about life, along with her journal denouncing slavery and the conditions on southern plantations had caused much controversy. Additionally, she was quite a blonde beauty, although she paled in comparison to Julia Toombs.

Julia felt privileged to be seated beside her at the Captain's table. The General's wife turned to her right. "Charlie Irving, my neighbor, and James Battle, one of our overseers, met you when you secretly occupied the slave quarters behind your ex-husband's mansion on Georgia's coast," she said. "Do you remember?"

A little startled at mention of her husband, Fanny thought quickly of something off-putting to say. "Of course, I remember. Those two had such a close bond for slave and landed gentry. I delighted in their company."

"Oh, Mrs. Butler, we don't call ourselves landed gentry in America. And James Battle was a free man before the war began."

"Still, he was once a slave," Fanny noted. "Freedom is not something that should be given. It should be a part of one's birthright."

"I never thought of it that way," Julia said. "Perhaps you're right. But what of those who are unprepared for their freedom and must be looked after?"

Fanny locked eyes with Julia. "There is no such thing as being unprepared for freedom. If freedom seems daunting to some former slaves, education can overcome all fears."

"But our slaves were educated," Julia retorted. "Both my father and my husband are great proponents of education. All of our slaves were well treated and taught to read and write."

Fanny leaned toward Julia. "I traversed most of Georgia researching slave conditions and I am aware that there were some plantations where slaves were well treated and educated. But these were bestowed as benign gifts, not rights."

"Yes," said Julia thoughtfully. "You are quite right. Perhaps one day all men will really be equal as the Constitution guarantees."

"And while your Constitution implies women, too," Fanny said, surveying the couples at the table, "I would hope that the word *women* would be inserted in that guaranty soon." A dead silence fell over the table at Fanny's remark, although a few of the women smiled.

Love Rises

***

The three women spent many days on deck. Cocooned in lap robes and plied with coffee by attendants, they chatted long hours about Fanny's stage career and Selena's ability to get whatever she wanted from men.

One afternoon Fanny turned to Julia. "You have little to say about your life, Julia. Tell us more."

"Oh, there is little to tell. We try to make it day to day. It's not like it was in the old days with flowers and parties and music all day long."

"And did you enjoy that frivolous life?" asked Fanny.

Julia looked thoughtful. "Actually, not as much as I enjoy scrounging for our livelihood."

"And what is the most interesting part of your life?" Fanny probed.

Julia answered without hesitation. "Love," she said, "and that includes a little Mulatto girl, an old colored woman and the man, James, who is the child's father. He has given his all to keep our plantation in Stewart County going and we reward him by selling it."

"Ancillary loves are always surprising but very rewarding," Fanny said, indicating to the attendant that the three women wanted more coffee. "Tell me more about the man and the Mulatto child. I am very much interested." The women talked on until the cold drove them to their staterooms.

***

With goodbye kisses for Fanny and Selena, Julia disembarked the *Alabama* and immediately boarded the *Creole*, bound for Mobile, her baggage and paintings now stowed in its hold.

***

Home to Washington, Georgia, December, 1865

James and Charlie stood on the dock as the *Creole* pulled into Mobile's harbor. Julia was one of the first passengers down the gangplank and she threw herself into Charlie's arms.

Remembering past injuries and fearful of her condition, Charlie held her gingerly.

"Please, Charlie. I'm not a china doll. Hold me."

Charlie laughed, swept her off her feet and swung her around. Julia joined in his laughter saying, "I said hold, not twirl."

They headed for the wagon. While James stowed Julia's luggage, Charlie helped her up saying, "We've made a bed of quilts for you in the back."

Julia stiffened. "How many times do I have to tell you I'm carrying a child, not an illness?" She seated herself and called to James. "James, please lay those portraits on the quilts. They need more care than I do. One is a special gift for Charlie."

"Yes ma'am," said James. "I was wondering what was in those wrappings. They'll rest easy there."

Charlie seated himself beside Julia and kissed her on the cheek. James took the reins and the unlikely three began their long journey home, watchful for Union troops.

Charlie turned toward Julia. "There have been some changes since you left. I don't know if the General told you he sold Roanoke. The new owner let James go."

"I knew Roanoke sold, but I didn't know you were displaced, James," Julia said, leaning over Charlie and putting a hand out toward the overseer who had served Roanoke well for many years. "You must bring Lily and come live with us."

"We're already there, Miss Julia," James responded. "And mighty glad of it."

Charlie interjected, "James and I built two cradles. Tilde stays in the house with baby Lily, and James and I live in the slave quarters."

"That'll give Euphemia plenty to talk about," Julia remarked.

"It makes sense, Julia; James and I will be up at dawn soon, planting corn and cotton seed at Greenway," Charlie said, referring to the Toombs' plantation closest to town.

"Where ever did you get the seed?"

"The seed was kind of a reward. Some of the owners on the coast were grateful for my part in retrieving their property. Planting's not the problem. The problem is that we can't possibly harvest the crops alone."

James said nothing, but looked thoughtful.

***

Each night before they camped, James rode ahead and scouted the site, alert for Yankees.

On the last day of the homeward journey, their wagon rounded a curve, and all three of them gasped. Ahead, they could see an obstruction set up by Union cavalry, blocking the road.

Charlie's first thought was for Julia. Before she knew what was happening, he had picked her up and placed her on the quilts with the paintings. "Cover up and try to look weary," he said.

"That won't be difficult," she said. Still, she took a piece of charcoal from her reticule, smudged it under her eyes and disarranged her hair. A little talcum powder served to make her pale. The Union officer came around the neatly stacked pile of branches interspersed with small tree trunks cut to a point that blocked the road. He demanded of Charlie, "What are you transporting here?"

Charlie stepped down from the wagon. "Just my wife who is with child. We are on the way home to Wilkes County for Christmas, Captain."

As the Union officer lifted the flap at the back of the wagon, Julia raised up on one elbow, a rounded pillow over her abdomen beneath the quilt. "Are we home, Charlie?" she asked in a quivery voice all the while thinking, If the Captain uncovers me or the nude portrait, we're dead.

The Captain had a wife and children of his own. He was sick to death of war and its aftermath that would stop a man and his pregnant wife simply because they were on their way home for the holiday. He raised an arm to his waiting soldiers. "Pass," he shouted.

Julia fell back on the quilts, careful not to disturb her portraits. She was glad of the comfort and fell asleep immediately.

***

By the time the wagon pulled into their hometown, Julia was awake and as carefully groomed as she could manage. Charlie's mother, Belle, heard the wagon and ran out to join them.

"Welcome home, son. I'll be over later with supper for all of you. I'd bring Drummer Boy, but that cat won't let me touch him."

Charlie swung down and gave his mother a hug.

Julia peered out of the wagons' cover. "Thanks so much, Mrs. Irving," she said. "We have a lot to unload and there's probably not enough food in the house for all of us. Drummer Boy will be along on his own, I'm sure."

"If he can avoid Euphemia. The two of them have a real cat and mouse game going, with Drummer Boy being the mouse."

Julia laughed. "I'm betting on Drummer Boy," she called as Charlie joined her and the wagon pulled away down The Row.

***

Charlie escorted Julia upstairs to rest and returned to unload the last of her luggage and the portraits while James tended the horses. Charlie thought about waiting for James to help him with the largest trunk. It was double decked inside and bound with brass and leather outside. He lifted a corner, figured the weight at about seventy pounds, and decided to do it himself.

Just as he set the red trunk on the ground in front of the steps, James arrived from the barn. Charlie straightened. "Now that only the portraits are left, you appear," Charlie said, putting a hand on his lower back, feigning injury.

James laughed. "I'd a bin happy to trade coolin' down those horses for the trunk."

Charlie leaped on the step at the back of the wagon. "Let's look at the portraits before we take them in."

The two climbed into the back of the wagon and untied the tarpaulin-wrapped painting of Julia with Drummer Boy.

"She's just as beautiful in paint as she is in reality," Charlie remarked.

"Drummer Boy, too," James said. "Look at that fur, begging you to stroke it."

"How like Julia to insert the holly. We gathered holly before making love by the fire."

"Stop reminiscing," James said. "She's waiting for you in the flesh upstairs."

"Right," said Charlie. "Let's unwrap the other portrait."

As the tarp came off the second painting, each man took in a long breath. "I suspect this one is the gift for you," James said, letting the air he had held for too long out of his lungs.

In a hoarse whisper Charlie spoke. "You better wrap this back up and take it to our quarters. I know you're anxious to see little Lily."

James turned to rewrap the nude picture of Julia, pausing to admire the sheen of her skin, the pinkness of her nipples, the thatch of dark hair between her thighs. "I'm no more in a hurry than you," James answered. But Charlie had already left.

***

Christmas was a merry affair on The Row. Although there was little money for gifts, there was much knitting of scarves, mittens and sweaters, and crocheting along the edges of handkerchiefs. There were wood carvings by those who had the talent. James made walnut pull toys for Lily and Lucy. Julia and Charlie always referred to the unborn babe by name so

James thought of her as baby Lucy, also. From an old banister, he fashioned a turtle for Lily, who could not yet walk, and a rabbit for Lucy who was scheduled to make her appearance in July.

In addition to the wooden box she left him before she went to Paris, Julia placed a sprig of holly bound with horsehair under the tree for Charlie. It was meant as a reminder of his gift, her nude portrait. He gave her a cream colored cameo set on onyx, framed in gold with tiny golden chains dangling on each side. Julia suspected the broach originally belonged to Charlie's mother, which could only mean that Belle knew about and approved of their union.

Charlie's father, Judge Elijah Battle, died in his sleep a few days after Christmas. A gentleman to the death, Julia thought. He purposely postponed his demise so it wouldn't interfere with the holiday.

During the long winter days that followed, Tilde and Julia took turns rocking Lily by the fire. By early March, James and Charlie rose at dawn to plough and plant.

James drove Gray Alice and Charlie drove Young Alice, plowing adjacent furrows in the rich land at Greenway. They paused at the end of a row and James raised an arm in allegiance to the acreage. "If there's enough rain, Charlie, I expect we'll see two thousand bales of cotton and a silo full of corn by early fall."

Charlie wiped his brow with a sleeve. "Sounds wonderful, but who's going to pick the corn and cotton? The two of us can't do it alone."

"I've been thinking, I have friends out there, Charlie."

"With those white-sheeted raiders marauding the countryside, I'd think every freedman would have cleared out to the North."

"A lot have gone," James said. "The raiders get more organized every month. By next year, I think they'll have leadership and a name. Then the burning and lynching will increase."

Charlie put a hand to his aching back. "Like I said, who's going to harvest the corn and pick cotton?"

James smiled. "The North doesn't have the only underground. Georgia's our state and some of us refuse to be driven out no matter what. Many are hidden, just waiting to emerge if someone offers a leg up. They'll help us. 'Course, we'll have to give them a share and house them."

"Glad to divvy up," said Charlie, motioning with the reins for Gray Alice to pull the plough. "I'll even give them back wages when the cotton sells. More than half of the slave quarters behind the houses on The Row are empty and nearly all that are close to plantations stand vacant. Our neighbors will offer shelter, and with a lot of hard work, Greenway will be crop-rich again."

***

James began to recruit harvesters from friends and friends of friends. He started just outside Savannah and worked his way home. He found them in shacks behind burned out plantation houses, camped in the woods, and even sleeping under bridges, ready to move instantly if they were warned of the KKK or others in the vicinity who wanted them dead. The scene was much the same for every encounter. Late at night James would arrive, bearing food and seed for those who still thought they could survive long enough to bring in a harvest of their own. He had a message for them. "Charles Irving is not like some you've known. He has leave to manage Greenway for Mrs. Toombs. We've already planted and come September, he will give you a share and back wages as soon as the cotton is sold. I give you Charlie's word, my word, and the word of General Toombs who owns the land. You'll have shelter and food. Bring any family members with you."

There were questions and some outright disbelief, but enough men to bring in the harvest were convinced. For months they came to The Row by night in twos and threes, sometimes in a much coveted wagon that transported their families. Some stayed in shacks behind deserted mansions outside of town. Others moved directly into empty mansions whose owners had fled for Texas and other faraway states.

Love Rises

Residents of The Row took the former slaves and their families in, fed and housed them behind The Row. Often, the freedmen and their loved ones were hidden in the cellars of the mansions when the KKK rode.

Chapter 10
Promise of Cotton and Corn

After the last frost melted, a riot of azaleas blossomed around houses on The Row, and the giant magnolia trees lining the lane to the Toombs' mansion budded. In the woods behind The Row, Dogwood trees burst into clouds of white among the evergreens.

At Greenway Plantation, corn sprang from the earth like tiny sprites waving toward the cotton fields where green stems topped with tight little bolls also pushed through the rich soil.

Love Rises

One sunny morning halfway through her pregnancy, Julia strolled down the lane with Lily in her arms, talking to her as if she was an adult. As they walked, Lily made comments. "Ah," she cooed. "Blowee."

"I know women in confinement aren't supposed to be seen, Lily, but it's such a glorious day, I think we'll not stay hidden in the lane but walk proudly down The Row."

"Oh," said Lily. Taking the baby's comment for approval, Julia stepped out of the lane and headed for Euphemia Foscue's stately home.

When they arrived, Euphemia was engaged in trying to trap Drummer Boy one more time. This time she wielded a tattered piece of tarp. As she threw the tarp over Drummer Boy, who was lapping up a saucer of milk, Julia's "Good Morning, Mrs. Foscue," was simultaneous with Drummer Boy shedding the tarp like a Selkie's skin, then bounding off to find sanctuary under Dattie Tucker's front steps.

Abandoning her failure, Euphemia responded to Julia. "Julia. Please come in. You shouldn't be seen in your condition. What would the General say?"

"I've already been seen, Euphemia, and the General isn't here to say anything."

Seated at the tea table, Euphemia passed Julia a delicate cup of hot liquid, tinted by black tea. "Please put that child on the floor, Julia. Why must you carry her around like she is yours? Everyone knows she's a Mulatto. I shudder to think how she got that way."

"Lily is quite comfortable in my arms. I'm sure she got 'that way' in the usual way."

Euphemia huffed. "Imagine. A white child with a Negro father."

"You don't have to imagine, Euphemia. Lily is right here and she's as white as you are and as blonde as you once were."

At Julia's remark, Euphemia gave up and changed the subject. "About Drummer Boy, I was trying to capture him so that I could return him to you. I don't like him prowling around my property."

"Then," said Julia, taking a tiny sip of tea, "you should stop feeding him so that he will cease prowling."

Euphemia sniffed. "There's something peculiar about that cat of yours."

Julia smiled. "Yes. There is." As Julia and Lily rose to leave, Julia added, "There is more than one definition of peculiar, Euphemia. I think Drummer Boy is just peculiarly intelligent."

At the door, Euphemia recovered her manners. "Do stop in again, Julia."

"Lily and I will do that, won't we Lily?" Julia said.

Lily turned in Julia's arms and focused her light blue eyes on Euphemia. "No," she said clearly, shaking her blonde curls from side to side.

Love Rises

***

In late spring, Julia wrote to her husband in Paris:

My dearest Bob,

How we all miss you here. Charlie and James work at Greenway from dawn 'til dusk while Tilde and I mind James's daughter, Lily, and keep the household going.

It is a strange and meager life. Much time is spent in foraging for necessities. We two women could not manage without Charlie and James. At least there is water and plenty of wood. James says he has friends he can call on to harvest in the early fall. Could you possibly make arrangements in Paris for the sale of the cotton? James figures about 2,000 bales. As you know, he was never wrong about the crop at Roanoke. Please write soon and try to enjoy Paris. When do you think it will be safe for you to return home? I would very much enjoy your presence here before Lucy is born in July.

Your loving wife,

Julia

In a little over a month, Julia received a reply:

My darling black-eyed girl,

How lonely it is for me here as the Chestnut trees bloom and Parisians alight in the cafes like butter-flies to gardens. I take no pleasure in seeing the sights or dining without you. Solace lies in knowing Charlie and James are there to see to your needs.

Long staple is much sought after here and I am promised a good price for the cotton. Since the blockade was lifted, few plantations have produced enough to export. This sale should provide for our immediate future and the child to come.

I leave for Canada soon and will spend as much time there as needed for my safety. You may expect my address as soon as I know it. You will be happy to know that through circuitous channels, a meeting with President Johnson is being arranged on my behalf. My fervent hope is that I will come to you soon. I long to see your portrait over the mantel in our parlor and have our things about me. I yearn to see the townspeople gather in our yard upon my return. As unofficial Ambassador of the Confederacy here in Paris, I shall tell them about the staunch feelings for the South that still abound in Europe. Your loving,

Bob

Chapter 11
Two Births, Three Fathers

In the evenings, Charlie and Julia took the carriage out to view the crops.

"Isn't it glorious, Charlie?" Julia enthused. "Look what you've done."

Charlie helped her down and she leaned over to pick a tiny bud which already showed a bit of white.

"I should have accomplished nothing without James." Julia handed Charlie the cotton bud. He ran his finger over its tip, sniffed it, and looked out across the fields. They were both silent for a while, then Charlie said, "Those white-sheeted raiders have a name now. They call themselves the Ku Klux Klan. If they ever find out about our arrangement with James, they would burn us out and probably lynch him."

"But surely, Charlie, they mean only to get rid of Negro planters, not plantation owners and the freedmen who help them."

"They attack not only all Negros but Negro sympathizers as well."

"Just because we support a man who has always had our best interests at heart and he happens to be a different color?"

"You know in your heart what's true, Julia. They don't care what kind of man James is. The Klansmen would find it abhorrent that we are willing to give him a home and a share of this bounty." He gestured toward the fields before he took Julia's hand and helped her into the buggy. "Our Red Persuader Brigade is too small to have any effect on them."

When she was seated, Julia pulled her lace shawl around her, laid her head on Charlie's shoulder and said tremulously, "I fear for us, but I fear most for Lily."

Charlie put an arm around Julia and held her close. With a slight pull on the reins, he indicated that Charger should head for home.

Julia could feel the tension in his arm. "Why are you so tense, Charlie? Is it Lily?"

"Yes. I fear for Lily, too. But it's everything. I cannot

bear the thought of sharing you with the General when he comes home."

"It is not my wish either, but surely you can see we mustn't be enemies. We need each other. The General is selling the cotton crop in Paris which will allow for another planting."

"Those are practical matters, Julia," he said as he flicked the reins for Charger to move faster. "I feel that if I share you with another man, I'll be no better than a handler for a camp follower. No real man would allow such an alliance with the woman he loves."

Julia sat up straighter and Charlie's arm released her. "That's the old life. If we want to survive and keep even a semblance of our former lives, we must make drastic changes."

"I know, my love. I just don't know if I can be part of that kind of change."

Julia's dark eyes flashed. "We must do this to-gether. By all that we hold dear, there is no other way. Chivalry is dead. You must grow up, Charlie. Be the man who loves me, and meet this challenge."

Charlie's shoulders slumped. "I don't know if I can, Julia." They traveled in silence for a while.

Julia looked at Charlie but his attention was on the road. "You can if you want me and our child. Your feelings and mine come after our baby. And, are you forgetting Lily?"

"No," said Charlie as they arrived at the Toombs' mansion. "I'll defend you, our baby, and Lily to the death." Charlie jumped down and held out his hand to help Julia from the carriage.

"That's my soldier." Julia smiled, picked up her skirts, and started up the steps alone, in a fiercely determined manner. When she reached the veranda, she turned and called to him. "Come join me in my bedroom. And bring Drummer Boy. He's probably under the stove in the kitchen."

After Charlie put Charger in the barn, he stopped by the kitchen. Knowing what was coming, Drummer Boy jumped on Charlie's shoulder. The two moved up the steps into Julia's bedroom where she lay naked with her knees drawn up and tilted outward. Drummer Boy knew something was amiss between the lovers, and he was determined to offer the extra effort he felt was needed. He gave Julia's breasts some powerful pats, then licked each of her nipples into erectness. Before Charlie thrust into her, Drummer Boy was cast aside. Insulted, Drummer Boy jumped into the wash bowl and decided to go to sleep instead of watching.

***

Flowers surrounded the houses on The Row. White and blue and pink hydrangeas were abundant. Fragrant summer gardenias hedged around Dattie Tucker's house. At Greenway, the corn grew higher and the cotton bolls were getting fuller. There was enough rain but not too much. The slave quarters were filled with freedmen eager to harvest the crops by late August or early September, and take some of the profits. Ibo had brought several worm-gear rollers that he had used in Africa to pull seeds from the cotton, just in case existing cotton gins were burned by the KKK.

***

Tilde made Lily a corn husk doll and spit on the ground when it was finished. With the doll under her arm, the tiny girl asked, "How do you spit, Tilde?"

"They's water in your mouth all the time. You jes' gather it up and spew it out," the woman explained, showing her.

After two tries, Lily spat at least two inches. "Why do you spit, Tilde?"

"Oh, you don't want to spit unless you is good an' mad or mo' likely if you is just finished with sumthin'."

"Papa James says I'm the spittin' image of my Mama. What kind of spittin' is that, Tilde?"

"That's the good kind of spittin', like when you split a tree into two parts that is the same or when you is so much like your mama that even your spit is the same as hers."

"I like both kinds of spittin', Tilde," said Lily formally.

"Did your papa ever tell you who yo' mama is, chile?"

"She's not a *who*, Tilde. She's dead; she died when I was born."

Tilde put her arms around Lily. "Yes. I know chile. We all starts dyin' the moment we is born. Don't you worry none about not havin' a mama. Julia is yo' mama now and there's three papas plus me to love you."

"That makes me a lucky girl," Lily said, and she skipped off to find whatever papa she could locate.

***

James made Lily a sling shot and taught her to shoot. The tiny blonde with the face of an angel would sit for hours under the chinaberry tree, picking up china-berries and shooting them into the azalea bushes. Her aim improved daily. Each time when she finished, she would find a mark and spit at it. Then she would go in search of Charlie, who was remark-ably good at finding sugar and making a sugar tit for her. If she couldn't find Charlie or James, she would lay her head on Drummer Boy's stomach and hum a little song that resembled "Dixie" while the cat purred and thumped his tail in time to her tune.

Late one afternoon, Julia found Lily singing to Drummer Boy. "Would you like to hear Lucy's heart beat and feel her move?"

"Yes! Yes!" Lily jumped up and ran to Julia, who

seated herself in a rocker by the fireplace and pulled up her blouse to reveal her stomach. Lily put her ear and a small hand on Julia's rounded abdomen.

Julia thought Lily's cheek against her bare skin felt like silk, which reminded her of Paris. "Do you hear Lucy? Can you feel her kick?"

'It's not Lucy," Lily said. "It's my baby." She ran outside to find Tilde again.

Julia rearranged her blouse as Charlie came into the kitchen. "Did you hear that? Lily says it's her baby."

"I did hear. It's probably just a little jealousy. I wouldn't worry about it if I were you. In truth, I am part you, so definitely don't worry about anything. I'll take care of any jealousy of Lily's."

***

In late June, Julia received a letter from her husband. During a face to face meeting with President Johnson, where Bob Toombs refused to pledge allegiance to the Union, his letter informed her that even under these circumstances, President Johnson had given his word that Robert Toombs would neither be arrested nor tried for treason upon entry to the United States. During their meeting, the President had pointed out that both the South and the North were war weary and treason did not seem to garner any interest on either side. Julia harbored the last line of the General's letter to her heart: "*I will be allowed to travel home with a little money."*

Julia placed her husband's letter among her lingerie and drew Charlie aside. "He's on the way home. He'll be here before Lucy is born."

Charlie rested his chin on Julia's head. "How could you possibly know that?"

She stepped away and looked at her lover. "Easily. Lucy and I will just wait until he arrives."

***

Early in the morning of July fourth, Julia turned to Charlie and shook his shoulder gently. "Charlie, it's time."

From the depths of a deep sleep, Charlie answered her clearly, "Time for what?"

"The baby, of course. Lucy will be here soon."

"Charlie jumped out of bed as if the sheets had scalded him. "Today? What can I do?"

Julia laughed. "You can hold my hand. Don't worry. I've been in labor for hours. As soon as it's light, go alert Dr. Coleman."

"I'll go now," Charlie said, anxious for something to do.

Julia grasped his hand and placed it on her stomach, which hardened under his touch. Charlie drew back his hand. "Oh. That feels terrible. I'll go fetch Dr. Coleman now," he said again.

"If you must," she said. "But Lucy won't come for a few hours."

"Julia, how can you be so calm?" he asked.

"I told you. I've done this before. Now, go get Dr. Coleman. I see a little light. And rouse Tilde and tell her to come to me."

Charlie kissed her and started to rush from the room, realized he wasn't dressed, and hurriedly pulled on shirt and trousers. He entered the room where Tilde and Lily were sleeping and placed a hand on Tilde's shoulder. Lately, Tilde slept lightly while waiting for Julia's time to arrive. She was on her feet before the words left Charlie's mouth.

As Charlie hit the middle step, the General spurred his horse down the lane. The older man dismounted and the two embraced on the bottom step as the General said, "How is she, Charlie?"

The younger man answered, "In labor. I'm going for the doctor." As Charlie ran to the barn for his horse, he shouted unnecessarily, "Stay with her."

"Forever," the General answered quietly and leapt up the steps like a man half his age.

At Julia's side, the General kissed her brow and spoke gently. "How is it, this time, my love?"

"Much easier. But I'm glad you're here. You always come through when there's a problem; when our children were born and when they died."

"The birth of a child is no problem, my black-eyed girl. We will all love this new life you call Lucy and be glad, although we will hold the memory in our hearts of our three children lost to us."

Julia gripped his hand. "I thank you for your pleasure in Lucy's advent and join you in the memory of our children in heaven. I think I will rest a little until the light is clear, then we can all greet Lucy."

The General, who normally took up most of the space in any room he entered, stamping and blustering about, tiptoed to the door and whispered tenderly, "I'll leave the door open. Call when you need me."

***

When Charlie arrived with Dr. Coleman, the physician asked both men to leave the room while he examined Julia. After a few minutes he stepped outside the door. In his black suit and starched cuffs that matched his hair, the doctor was confidently in charge. "All seems to be in order, but I should have been summoned earlier."

"I would have come after you even sooner," said Charlie. "But she didn't wake me. You know how she is."

"Indeed, I do," said Dr. Coleman.

The General placed a hand on the doctor's shoulder, as he looked at Charlie. "We all do," he said.

"Doctor," Julia called. "Lucy is ready."

The two men paced the hallway, passing each other in silence for about a half hour. When they heard a lusty cry, Charlie moved toward the door, but the General put out an arm to deter him. "There are things the doctor must do. We will only be in the way." Charlie resumed pacing and after a few minutes they heard a weaker cry.

Tilde emerged with Lucy. "What wonders the Lord has in his store!" she said, handing the child to the General. As Toombs beamed down at Lucy, and Charlie lifted the cloth to look at her blue, blue eyes, the doctor emerged with another, smaller baby. The tiny girl was making mewing sounds so like a weak kitten that Drummer Boy ran up the stairs to investigate. Charlie almost stumbled over the cat as Dr. Coleman handed him the second baby.

The General looked at Dr. Coleman. "Twins?" he asked.

But it was Charlie who answered. "Not exactly," he said, holding out the infant to the General. "This one has brown eyes and red hair." Without a word, Bob Toombs and Charlie exchanged babies.

"Paris," the General said.

Misunderstanding, Charlie beamed. "I think Paris is a beautiful name for a girl."

Doctor Coleman placed one hand on Charlie's shoulder and one hand on General Toombs' shoulder. "Gentlemen, give the babies to Tilde. I need to see you downstairs in the parlor."

***

When they were seated in the strong morning light

that left no corner of the parlor shaded, Dr. Coleman said, "Am I correct in assuming that both of you had relations with Mrs. Toombs during the beginning of her first trimester?"

Charlie and Bob Toombs answered a hearty *yes* in unison.

The doctor adjusted his silk cravat. "It is unusual but not impossible for two inseminations that occur at different times, and even by different men, to result in twins such as these."

"But how can that be?" asked Charlie as the General smiled an all-knowing smile.

The doctor explained, "Conception close together but not at the same time. One twin is often smaller and weaker and could be pronounced premature. The smaller baby will require extra care."

The General announced in a firm voice, "The smaller baby's name is Paris. Don't you agree, Charlie?" As Charlie nodded his assent, Toombs added, "She will get all the care she needs, and beyond."

James built yet another crib, and Paris was placed in Julia's room. But Paris did not thrive as Lucy did. The infant refused Julia's breast and was not happy with a wet nurse. Finally, Tilde said to Julia, "Give me the chile. Sometimes the old ways is best."

"We will all be so grateful if you can get more nourishment into her, Tilde. I fear for her life."

"Don't you worry none, Miss Julia," Tilde said as she left the room with Paris. "I'll have her up to Lucy's size in no time. Jes' don't ask me how."

Charlie brought Lucy into Julia's room and placed her in Paris' cradle.

"I hope we're doing the right thing," Charlie said. He kissed Julia on the forehead and said, "I'd trust Tilde with my life, but it's hard to trust her with Paris. No telling what she's up to."

"We have no choice," Julia said.

***

What Tilde was up to was killing a hog. She strung the hog up in the smokehouse and carved out a teat and part of the breast with a sizable butcher knife. Then she set the big iron wash pot on an open fire and boiled the makeshift bottle for several hours. She sent James to get Ophelia, the wet nurse. Together, Tilde and the younger woman stroked the milk out of Ophelia's breasts, enough for several babies.

Tilde took the homemade bottle with a stranger's milk to Paris. The old woman settled in a rocker by the unlit fireplace while Lily stood beside her and stroked Paris' ginger-colored hair. Occasionally, Lily would leave her post to kiss Paris' toes when they escaped the receiving blanket.

Whether it was due to the wet nurse's milk, Tilde's folk knowledge about hogskin bottles, or Lily's attention, Paris thrived on the arrangement and began to gain weight. Soon, Paris was ready for Ophelia's breast.

***

When the babies were a month old, General Toombs and Charlie met on the south veranda to discuss the future.

The General spoke first. "While it is difficult for both of us, we must make arrangements to share Julia's bed."

Charlie shifted uncomfortably in his wicker chair. "It certainly is more than difficult General. You wouldn't consider…."

"No, I would not," boomed the older man, immediately grasping Charlie's intent to leave him out entirely. Toombs took a deep breath. "However, since I must be out building my law practice and making speeches on behalf of our state, I will grant you the larger share of Julia's time: Monday through Thursday and whenever I am out of the city."

"That's more than fair," said Charlie, shocked at the General's generosity. "I will remove myself to my mother's home Friday through Sunday of each week."

The two men shook hands. Charlie rose to leave since it was Friday, and the General lit a cigar.

Lily appeared as if on cue. "Blow rings for me, Papa Gen, please, pretty please with sugar on it, blow smoke rings for me."

The General pulled his curly-haired darling into

his lap. "Anything for you, Lily girl. Let's see how big I can make them before they disappear." The General told himself that he preferred Lily to the twin babies because she could walk and talk, but even as he thought it, he knew it wasn't true. From the first time he saw her, Lily had tied a string to his heart and secured a place that could never be equaled by another child.

***

In Julia's bedroom, her husband slid into the warmth of Julia's bed and stroked the silkiness of the flesh-colored nightgown he had bought for her in Paris. He pulled first one strap and then the other down her shoulders and buried his face between her breasts, kissing the hollow there as he was accustomed. He circled her nipples with his thumbs until he could feel them tighten.

Julia ran her fingers through his red mane, now streaked with white, and asked, "I presume the arrangement has been made. How did Charlie take it?"

"Very well. No pistols, no sabers, just regret at the sharing and astonishment at my generosity."

Julia sat up, slid her nightgown off, and tossed it into the washbasin. "Don't talk as if I'm a slave at auction," she said. "After all, it was my idea."

The General parted her legs with his knee and moved his thumbs down. "I did what I thought you would want. Charlie will be here Monday through

Thursday, lodge at his mother's over the weekends, and spend any nights with you when I'm away."

"Fair enough," said Julia, falling back on the pillows and wrapping one leg around Bob Toombs' back as she had so many times in the past.

***

On Monday, the General left town for an unannounced period of time and Charlie joined Julia in her bedroom. Lucy slept in her crib by the window and Charlie slid between the same sheets that Julia's husband had left that morning.

"I was afraid I'd lost you forever," Charlie said as he gathered Julia in his arms and kissed her bare shoulders. Cautiously, he ran two fingers between her thighs and was surprised to find her already wet.

Julia could feel his caution and surprise. "Did you think I would change after Bob, after the babies? I want you as much as ever, maybe more." She threw back the covers and placed herself astride him. "You haven't changed," she said rocking back and forth, reveling in his firmness, "Why should I?"

At her remark, Charlie sat up, lifted her onto the washstand and went to the door to let in Drummer Boy who was meowing to enter. "Remember the first time?" he asked as he returned. Julia smiled and opened her legs as he poured tepid water from the pitcher over her breasts. When he cupped them with his hands and opened his mouth, Charlie could hear

Drummer Boy lapping up the water pooled on the floor.

For reasons he didn't understand, the lapping sound sent Julia into a primal, fever pitch of movement that threatened to overturn the washstand. Charlie was astonished to realize that he could steady the washstand and meet Julia's every movement with perfect timing while managing not to step on the cat. Further, he was amazed that their union was even better this time than the first time.

***

While Julia and the twins were sleeping on a night when the moon was full, Charlie and James were roused by shouting and the smell of burning timber.

Six men on horseback, dressed in sheets with pointed hats, slits cut out so they could see, trampled the front lawn. Burning torches were held high above their heads and a blazing cross was planted near the steps.

Charlie and James had long since prepared for this event, and stepped onto the balcony where they had secreted buckets of sweetgum balls, a tin of kerosene, and two sling shots. The two men rapidly dipped sweetgum balls in kerosene, lit them with matches from their pockets, and rained fire on the marauders. Three of the intruders spurred their horses and left immediately, fearing a fiery death. The other three continued to circle and shout invectives: "Nigger lover! Traitor!"

"Thank God the General's out of town," Charlie said as he dipped a sweetgum ball in the kerosene. "He'd probably try to talk them away." James was too busy aiming to answer.

Never one to miss an adventure, Lily came out with a pail full of chinaberries and her slingshot. She placed herself on the third step from the bottom and got off two shots before the KKK leader and Charlie saw her at the same time.

"It's Lily," Charlie said as he and James rushed for the door that led to the balcony.

Stung by one of Lily's chinaberries, the leader urged his horse past the steps, then swooped down and gathered her like she was a bundle of kindling.

"Let me go," she screamed at the same time Charlie shouted for James to get the shotgun.

"Why should I let you go?" the Klansman teased, "What would your papa do if I took you home with me?"

"I have three papas and one of them's a general. They would come after me."

"Yessiree," answered the Klansman, and one of your papas is a nigger."

Lily looked up at him. "I don't know what that is, but it's three will shoot you, sword you, and bury you." Lily had had enough at this point and she gathered up all the liquid in her mouth. With true aim, she spit into the triangular slit cut in the pointed hat and hit the eye of the Klan leader.

"Why you little spitfire," he raged, wiping his eye with the sheet. Then he looked down at the diminutive bundle who seemed unfazed by his superior strength or the danger she was in, and laughed a hearty laugh, amazed that this Mulatto child had captivated him. As James came out with a shotgun, the Klansman swept past the steps and deposited Lily where he had found her. The other two horsemen threw their burning torches onto the porch and fled. As if agreed, James plucked Lily off the step and carried her into the house while Charlie stomped out the still blazing torches.

When Charlie returned to Julia's bed, she inquired sleepily, "Why are you up?"

"Just checking on Drummer Boy," he said.

Julia thought this was peculiar since Drummer Boy was asleep in the washbasin, but she was too tired to inquire further. She moved into Charlie's arms and was asleep again moments after she placed her head on his shoulder.

***

The next morning Lily followed Tilde, Paris in one arm, as she went to the kitchen door to admit Ophelia. "I shot and spit at some bad men last night, Tilde," she said.

"Lord, chile, what dreams you has," Tilde said,

handing over Paris to Ophelia. As Ophelia settled into a rocker to nurse Paris, Tilde took Lily on her lap. "Now, tell us the story of you and the bad men."

"Paris and I want to hear, too," said Ophelia, as she palpitated her breast so that the baby could get more milk.

"Well," said Lily, "the bad men were big and white. I shot at them and spit at them and Papa James and Papa Charlie shot at them…"

At that point in her story, Drummer Boy entered the kitchen and took up his post under the stove. He nodded as Lily told her tale even though he had a different perspective. Last night, Drummer Boy had returned from digging in the woods to find Charlie stamping out a fire on the veranda and Lily being carried into the house by James. Then Drummer Boy saw Charlie remove the burned thing from the lawn along with the burnt sticks on the veranda. Afterwards, Charlie brought a bucket of water and scrubbed the porch and poured the rest on the lawn where the burned thing had been.

Drummer Boy thought for the hundredth time that people were peculiar. Why would they want to burn each other up, he wondered as he went to sleep, happy that he had not been a target. He liked the warmth from the stove, but he had never liked fire.

***

The next evening, while the moon was still full,

Drummer Boy set out for Dattie Tucker's house, ever vigilant for Euphemia's traps. Today, there was no food, no basket or pail ready to trap him. Euphemia was not in the porch rocker pretending to knit. Drummer Boy crept cautiously up the steps, onto the porch, and peered into the front window. He could see past the parlor into the kitchen where pieces of a broken plate and several minnows lay scattered on the floor. All he could see of Euphemia was one foot which pointed toward the kitchen ceiling. Then he picked up her scent and began to yowl long, shuddering cries that brought Dattie Tucker running to see what was wrong.

***

The Presbyterian Church stood pristinely just off the square. Parishioners had kept its white, clapboard sides clean even during the war. The steeple still pointed to heaven and its stained glass windows remained untouched.

The citizens of Washington, Georgia were grateful that their little town was located too far off Sherman's march of destruction to the sea for him to alter his route. For this reason alone, the church and the residences of Washington, Georgia were still standing.

Euphemia was given a lovely, flower-filled funeral at the church, although she was not a member, nor could she claim one real friend among the townspeople who crowded into the sanctuary. Still, the Reverend Jonathan Clifford did his best: "Euphemia Foscue was a longtime member of this community," he said in closing. "She kept abreast of affairs in Washington, and it is our responsibility that she goes on to her reward with our blessing." Eyebrows were raised in wonder at just what the hereafter's reward might be for the town busybody.

Drummer Boy meowed his assent to the preacher's words as he looked down the pew at Tilde, Lily, and the wet nurse Ophelia, who held both babies in her ample arms. Only Drummer Boy cried when they all marched row by row to the churchyard for Euphemia's interment.

Around the perimeter of the cemetery, former slaves who remained in the community burst into a rendition of "There is a Balm in Gilead" that began quietly and finally overcame the sound of the bells tolling from the church tower.

***

Without an adversary he could best, Drummer Boy seemed to lose his zest for life. He no longer joined Dattie Tucker in digging for the lost Confederate gold. She did her best to coax him, but he would not go into the woods with her on nights when the moon was full. Further, he rarely joined Charlie and Julia when they made love. While the lovers were inventive, it was as if he had watched them so many times that he no longer found their couplings of interest.

One afternoon when the light was fading in the bedroom, Charlie placed Drummer Boy on Julia's naked breasts. The cat pawed them gently, but not with any enthusiasm, so that Julia remained unaroused.

"I guess Drummer Boy is getting old, and I'll have to take over," Charlie mused.

Julia moved the cat to her side and opened her arms to Charlie. "I think you're right, my love, but I shall miss him."

"Strangely enough, so will I," Charlie said with no small amount of wonderment.

As if in atonement for Drummer Boy's lack of interest, the two made love in quiet contentment, then lay back to discuss their future.

They lay on their sides, face to face with arms around each other. Charlie looked into Julia's eyes and stroked her long, dark hair. "I would never have thought I could settle into sharing you with another man."

Julia raised up on one elbow. "What sharing? Bob Toombs is always out doing what he does best: making speeches, getting involved in politics over the state, and womanizing every chance he gets."

"You can't be sure about the women," Charlie said.

"Yes. I can. We females have networks you men can never imagine. Tilde has a friend who works for one of his conquests. She sent word to Tilde that Bob not only spent several nights with the woman, but was involved in a drunken brawl after a political meeting."

Charlie pulled her down to his bare chest. "The good thing is that he's gone most of the time."

Julia sat up and pulled the sheet around her. "Which means you and James do all the work plus most of the fathering around here."

"The General does his part. He supplies a lot of the money that keeps Greenway going. And you know that both James and I can't get enough of parenting these girls."

Julia lay back on the pillows and stared out the window. "I worry about Lily. What's going to happen to a Mulatto girl in the South when it's time for her to marry?"

Charlie thought back to the night of the KKK attack. "I wouldn't worry too much about Lily. Times must change and she's just the one to change them." He often thought that because of Lily, the crops were not burned and they were never attacked by the Klan again.

Julia sighed. "Lily will be a hundred years old before she's accepted by southern society."

Charlie took Julia into his arms with vigor, signaling that more aggressive love making was in store. As she raised her arms and gripped the bedposts, Charlie moved his hardness against her thigh. "I'm betting on Lily," he said, parting her legs.

Julia found she couldn't answer as she placed her feet flat on the sheet and slid onto him.

Chapter 12
The Little Girls

In the summer, just before the twins were three years old, Lily stood on the bottom step with the younger girls just above her, conducting a class. "This is the letter A for apple," she said, holding up a drawing she had made. The twins nodded. "And this is M for mother," she said, holding up a daguerreotype of Julia she had taken from the big dresser in Julia's room. "Yes," chorused the twins. "Mother." Then she held up a Y. "What begins with this letter?" she asked. "Yan-kee," the girls said. "What kind of Yankee?" Lily asked. "Vile Yankee," the girls screamed.

Charlie heard this invective as he approached from

the barn. "That's enough, girls," he said. "Not all Yankees are vile."

"Papa Gen thinks they are," Lily said, chin raised, ready for an argument.

"Sometimes Papa Gen thinks larger and harder than he should," Charlie said.

Lily shook her blonde curls in agreement. "It's probably just the whiskey talking," she said.

Charlie could think of nothing to add to Lily's comment so he patted the ginger hair of Paris and the dark hair of Lucy, and moved past them up the steps. When he entered the door and started up the winding staircase to Julia's room, he thought he and Julia must discuss an agreement to watch what they said in front of Lily.

On the steps outside, Lily said, "School's over, let's go play in the woods."

The three joined hands and ran for the patch of wildflowers where they knew they would find butterflies and maybe a ladybug or two. Later, they would go to the kitchen and ask Tilde to give them milk and cookies. Treats were plentiful because times were good. Even at four and a half, Lily knew this. She still had a faint memory of hunger and tea with a few drops of milk that had served as her breakfast when she was much younger.

"Alright, now let's go to the kitchen. Tilde will give you a jar for your ladybug, Lucy."

"But I don't have a bug." Paris complained.

"Very well," Lily said like an indulgent parent. "I will find you one."

***

On a hot morning in August, Lily came into the kitchen late and took a roll from the breadbox. She sat down on the floor by the stove where Drummer Boy spent most of the day.

She ate her bread silently and then said, "Do you want to learn your ABC's, Drummer Boy, or would you rather sing?" She reached out to pat him but he felt different. Drummer Boy was stiff and did not respond to her touch. When she pulled him from under the stove, Drummer Boy looked at her with half open, blank eyes. Lily had never seen a dead cat but she realized that Drummer Boy's feisty spirit was gone. "Tildeee," she screamed.

But it was Julia who ran into the kitchen, comforted Lily, threw the rolls into the kitchen sink, and placed Drummer Boy's body in the ornate, wooden breadbox.

Charlie entered from the back porch and took the sobbing Lily in his arms. Lucy and Paris came into the kitchen quietly and Charlie gathered them up as well. He sat in the rocker with a twin on each knee, holding Lily between them.

Julia sat in the other rocker and addressed them. "Girls, we will have a lovely funeral with flowers and words for Drummer Boy, today."

"Let's make it at dusk," Charlie said. "There's a full moon tonight and that would please him."

Lily wiped her tears. "Lucy, Paris, let's sit at the kitchen table and make funeral notices to deliver to The Row."

Julia and Charlie looked at each other. Both were astonished that Lily even knew about funeral notices. "We'll help," said Charlie as Julia drew out parchment and black ribbon from a bottom drawer and laid them on the table.

***

The girls walked straight-backed and somber, in single file down the lane to Dattie Tucker's house. Lily knew the old lady and Drummer Boy were close, so she reasoned Dattie Tucker should be the first to receive the rolled parchment tied with black ribbon which announced the place and hour of Drummer Boy's funeral. Lucy took one of the invitations from the basket over Lily's arm and laid it just outside the threshold. Lily lifted Paris so that she could use the door knocker. The three girls did not wait for a response, as they had at least an hour's trek ahead of them before they could return to the comfort of their three fathers, their mother, and Tilde.

Chapter 13
Drummer Boy's Legacy

Just before dusk, Charlie, James, Julia, and the General all lit kerosene lamps, and with the little girls, headed for the woods behind the mansion. Only Charlie and James carried shovels over their shoulders. The General carried the breadbox that held Drummer Boy's body. Lily carried a small wooden cross. Paris and Lucy had picked wildflowers, now wilted, and filled tiny baskets which they held against their hearts.

"What do you think, James?" asked Charlie as the two began to dig. "About four feet by four feet and two feet deep?"

Before James could answer, the General spoke. "Oh, give the animal some room. We have lots of space. How about six feet long by four wide and four deep?"

"Yours to command, General," said Charlie and the two began to dig at the soft earth in earnest as Dattie Tucker and Charlie's mother, Belle, arrived. No one else from The Row bothered to attend a cat's funeral.

As the sun sank below the horizon, a pale yellow moon rose above the treetops. Julia held her lantern high as Lucy and Paris walked the perimeter of the gravesite distributing wilted flowers. "Careful girls."

"Yes, mama," they answered in unison.

At that moment, Tilde arrived with a spade. "Come here, chile, let's plant your cross at the head of Drummer Boy's grave." Lily gave a little sob and joined her.

The heavy scent of Georgia soil filled the air as Charlie and James dug furthur into the soft earth. James was faster than Charlie, so as they came near their depth, Charlie reached out his arms. "Hand me Drummer Boy's coffin."

"He was a good cat," said the General.

"He certainly was," Julia and Charlie chorused as Charlie reverently placed the wooden box in the grave.

Twang. James' shovel struck metal, alerting the group.

Remembering the many nights she had spent digging for Confederate treasure with Drummer Boy, Dattie Tucker was first to jump into the grave, followed in quick succession by the other adults who surrounded the pit. Julia was last. Before she jumped, she handed her lantern to Lily.

Obeying their mother's admonition for caution, the three little girls hovered at the edge. Lily shone her lantern on the adults. James began to make a trench fast and furiously around the metal.

"Ahhh," breathed the group as a box was revealed. Then a collective "Ohhh," escaped them as James uncovered two more strongboxes.

The General said in a reverent whisper, "Somehow I knew this trench needed to be longer and deeper."

Dattie bent over and kissed the wooden coffin. "I always knew you'd find the gold, Drummer Boy. I knew you'd find it for us."

The digging continued silently until James set two boxes along the side of the gravesite and Charlie placed the third near the foot of the grave.

"What's in the boxes, Papa?" Lily asked, directing her question to any one of the three fathers who might answer.

"Let's see, daughter of mine," said James who used the corner of the shovel to knock off the lock and pry up the lid of one of the boxes marked "Confederate States of America."

In the dim light of the moon, heightened by four

flickering lanterns, hundreds of gold coins shone with a brilliant, almost touchable gleam. A gleam that only gold offers.

Paris, who usually said very little, commented. "Pretty."

***

Late that night when the little girls were in bed, Charlie, Julia, James, the General, Belle, Dattie, and Tilde gathered in the parlor like conspirators. All were seated except for Tilde who stood off the parlor almost in the dining room.

"Sit down, Tilde," ordered Julia.

"Don't seem fittin'," said Tilde.

Julia looked over her shoulder at Tilde. "Neither is digging up gold and stashing it under the stove."

"Sit," said the General. Tilde pulled a chair out from the dining table and sat.

Accustomed to running forums, the General began, "We shall run this democratically, with each of us casting a vote."

"Majority rules," said Charlie. All nodded and *ahemed* agreement.

The General's deep voice filled the parlor. "What to do with the gold? I estimate close to a million."

Dattie said, "We could place a statue of Drummer Boy in the square."

The General straightened, dismissing her idea. "I said a million."

"We could split it seven ways," said James, looking around the group.

"That doesn't seem equitable since Charlie and I are mother and son," Belle pointed out.

"We won't charge you for that, Belle," the General said as if he had consulted a set of rules in his head.

"We could buy more land," said Julia. "Not all plantations have been fortunate enough to have managers that even come close to Charlie or James. There's plenty of land for sale at very good prices."

Charlie stood up. "I say yes to the land and we give a share to all the freedmen who helped us harvest. Without them Greenway would not have survived, much less prospered."

The General stood as well. "That's well and good for James who managed Roanoke and Greenway, but to give property to cotton pickers?" The General raised his voice. "No. I won't have it." He shouted, "Tilde, bring me a bottle of whiskey," leaving the room, red-faced, his boots sounding like hammers as he went up the stairs.

"I like the idea of deeding land to the freedmen," proffered Dattie, followed by Belle and James.

Julia reinforced the others. "The freedmen should definitely be rewarded. We should all have a portion of the gold; you, too, Belle. And Dattie, there will be plenty left over for a statue of Drummer Boy in the square. You, James, will get your share of the gold even though the General seems to have relegated you to a place with the other freedmen. You should have the same acreage they receive as well as your gold."

James started to protest and Charlie held up a hand to stop him. "Julia, do you think you can do anything to change the General's mind about giving property to the freedmen?"

"I can try," said Julia. "But not until morning. He'll take that bottle to bed and drink until he loses consciousness."

Chapter 14
Death Changes Life

For the first time, Charlie and Julia made love under the same roof as the General. They clung together like survivors from a shipwreck, rocking their bed like a plank in the ocean, hardly giving a thought to their new riches.

At dawn, Julia went down to the kitchen, made a pot of coffee, and placed it with two porcelain cups on a silver tray which she brought to the General's room. She sat on the side of the bed and shook his shoulder. "Bob, Bob. It's Julia." But he didn't respond. She lay two fingers on his neck and grasped his wrist with her other hand. Stunned, she collected herself for a moment. Then she kissed his brow, folded his arms across his chest and made the sign of the cross as was the custom. She sat on the edge of the bed for a few more moments with the body of her husband, reflecting on the good times during their marriage.

Quietly, she rose from the bed and took the tray into the other room. She poured a cup of coffee for herself and one for Charlie. As the steam spiraled upward from the twin cups, Charlie rose on one elbow. "He's dead Charlie." To her surprise, a sob escaped her lips.

Charlie leapt up and held her in his arms until her sobbing ceased. Pouring water from the pitcher on the washstand into the basin, Julia washed her face and prepared to meet the day as the widow of General Robert Augustus Toombs.

***

Word traveled fast after Charlie roused Dr. Coleman to come pronounce the General dead. Mourners stood three deep on the lawn. All were silent and all were dressed in black. Some of them were Negros from Wilkes County, others were pillars of the community. People from all walks of life came from surrounding counties.

While General Toombs was a drunk who was accused of cheating at cards in college, he was also generous with his time and money and a stalwart supporter of the state of Georgia. He treated everyone fairly, regardless of station in life. Many citizens of Washington, Georgia were beholden to him for staving off disaster, both personal and financial.

The General lay in an open coffin at his home for three days so that a contingent from Washington, D.C. who remembered his days as a gifted orator in the U.S. Senate, could arrive to pay their respects. President Johnson sent his regards and sympathy to the widow by way of two emissaries from his office.

***

No church could accommodate General Toombs' mourners, so the service was held out of doors in the cemetery adjoining the Presbyterian Church. The heavens opened for the great man's funeral and rain pelted the crowd. A sea of black umbrellas filled the cemetery and flanked the length of its wrought iron fence. Those with umbrellas sheltered mourners who were unprepared or didn't own an umbrella.

When Julia stepped from the carriage in her golden dress which the General had bought from the House of Worth in Paris, there was an audible gasp from the crowd at her lack of decorum. Dattie Tucker nudged the woman beside her. "She looks like a dark angel in that dress," she said. "You do know there are dark angels? Not all angels are blonde." The woman looked at Dattie, straightened her black felt hat, set it dead center on her head, and said nothing.

Julia nodded to the crowd, refused a small umbrella, and said in a clear voice, "This dress was his last gift to me." She opened her matching fan and held it overhead for cover as rain plastered the gown to her curvaceous body. The crowd parted as she went to stand beside Charlie and Belle, who waited at the General's coffin with a giant black umbrella. Charlie could barely restrain himself from taking a shivering Julia in his arms.

The Reverend Clifford began his sermon. "I don't know what to say." No wonder, Julia thought. She knew that she was the only one who had ever fully understood the General: a pompous, overbearing, generous, understanding man with a penchant for liquor and women. She looked at the coffin covered with magnolia blossoms that befitted a southern gentlemen. Julia wondered where the ivory blossoms had come from as they were all long dead in Wilkes county.

After the funeral, Charlie, Belle, and Julia secluded themselves in the Toombs' mansion. No one gossiped because Belle was ever present. Without a spoken agreement, the residents of The Row closed ranks and refused to acknowledge Julia and Charlie's affair because all of them loved and respected the lovers who, after all, were also residents of The Row.

***

In the parlor, the will was read to Julia, Charlie, and Belle by the General's law partner. When the attorney said the words: *My homestead on The Row I leave to my stalwart friend, Charles E. Irving, who once saved my life. All real property that remains, including Greenway Plantation, I leave to Miss Lillian Battle, excepting the income from Greenway, which I leave to my beloved wife, Julia DuBose Toombs.*

After the stunned group saw the lawyer to the door, Belle said, "I'll leave you two to digest the General's wishes."

Julia and Charlie retired to their bedroom. Lying fully clothed on the bed, they held each other.

Charlie spoke first. "You are now a woman without property but at least with the gold and the income from Greenway, you're rich and can buy another plantation. I can't believe I own your house."

"Oh Charlie, can't you see what he intended was to keep us all together," she said, her voice filled with admiration.

Charlie pulled Julia closer. "He was always good at that, far better than I," Charlie said as he unbuttoned her blouse, unhooked her corset, pulled down her pantalets and freed her body. He ran his hands over every curve, kissed her lips and the hollow of her neck. "I've never made love to a rich woman."

"I'll help you," said Julia. She unbuttoned his trousers, pulled them down and knelt beside him, her full lips slightly open.

Love Rises

***

For three weeks, Belle, Charlie, Julia, and James made plans, located and bought plantations and had them surveyed. Blocks of one hundred acres each were deeded to the freedmen who had saved Greenway. James had gathered them all in the parlor at the Toombs' mansion. Some stood, some sat gingerly on the upholstered furniture. Others were more comfortable cross legged on the carpet.

James was the first to speak. "In recognition of your service to Greenway and your allegiance to the state of Georgia, we present each of you with one hundred acres of prime Georgia land." He passed out the deeds.

There was a murmur of disbelief over the crowd. Ibo, from the Butler Plantation, rose. He had sheltered James and helped with recovery of property along the coast. In addition to helping with the harvest at Greenway, Ibo had brought several worm-gear rollers to extract seeds from the cotton. The giant freedman, who stood at just under seven feet, addressed Charlie and James. "Do you mean that we should sharecrop this property?"

"Look at the deed," Charlie said. "Each of the hundred acre plots is in your respective names."

James surveyed his friends and fellow freedmen. "You are to do as you wish with your own property, recorded in the proper counties in your names. You may sell it or plant and work it or give it to another."

This news was met with silence and a few tears, then glee. Finally, Ibo shouted, "Lord God Almighty, we've been delivered from Armageddon and Heaven has come to us." As each man left, he was presented with a small sack of gold which held enough coins to buy seed, a plow, and a mule.

Chapter 15
The Drummer Boy Ball

When her mourning period was over, Julia sent out invitations to the Drummer Boy Ball. The theme was feline and each guest was to bring a cat if they owned one.

The Drummer Boy Ball would always be remembered as the hit of the season. The whole town of Washington, Georgia was invited, and a band from New Orleans was on the balcony to greet guests as they arrived. Hundreds of candles lit the house and tables were laden with seafood, cheese grits, and fruit. There was a separate dessert table featuring pecan pie and other southern sweets. Champagne flowed from Tilde's deft hand to hundreds of crystal glasses on a table in the stair hall. On the back porch, bowls of peeled shrimp were set out for the cats.

Dattie Tucker arrived with an orange tom cat around her neck. Felines of all colors and sizes came in the arms of guests and sometimes under both arms of a guest. An Englishman in a top hat sportively brought a Siamese cat on a leash. Although the cat was undocumented, he was the first feline of his breed to arrive in America.

Emboldened by her new found riches, Dattie sidled up to the Englishman as he handed his top hat to Tilde. "My Goldie has taken a liking to your interesting looking cat," she said, stroking Goldie's fur. "Shall we take them out to dine together on the back porch?"

"Jolly good idea," replied the Englishman. He set the Siamese on his shoulder, wrapped the leash around his wrist and offered Dattie his arm. "My name is Sir Arthur Whiffingham."

Dattie leaned in. "I'm Dattie," she confided in a conspiratorial whisper: "Only the residents of The Row know this party is an engagement announcement."

"The Row?" he said. "I don't understand. Will you enlighten me, Miss Dattie?"

"With pleasure," Dattie answered as she moved closer to Sir Arthur. She had heard that Europeans liked plump, older women.

**

Just before the guests were scheduled to arrive, Julia looked everywhere for Charlie but couldn't find him. Complete with curls atop her head, she was dressed in a new red velvet gown. Julia sat at her dresser, where the candles in sconces at the side of the mirror lit her face and made her eyes shine.

Charlie entered with a large package under his arm and caught sight of Julia in the dresser's mirror. "You are so beautiful," he said.

Julia turned. "Wherever have you been, my love?"

"Putting things to rights," he said, leaning the tarp-covered object against the far side of the bed. He pulled hammer and nails from his back pocket and pounded two nails into the wall over the bed with a vengeance. Then he tore off the tarp and hung the portrait of Julia's nude body over the bed.

Julia laughed and held out her arms to him. He lifted her onto the dresser, then pulled the red dress to her waist. She wore no undergarments. As the two fell into a world of their own, the hammer fell from Charlie's pocket. The loud blow sent a crack across the center of the white marble surface of the dresser.

When they were finished, Julia stood up, pulled on her dress and said primly, "Our guests will be arriving soon." Then she noticed the crack in the marble and laughed. "We'll have to make up a story about that crack."

"How about I carried it out and threw it on the lawn to save it during a fire started by the KKK?"

"We won't be married for six more months," Julia pointed out. "So the heroism will have to lie with the General."

"Fair enough," said Charlie. "He was always fair with me."

"The General always liked a perfect story," Julia said, locking arms with Charlie. "Now, let's go downstairs and greet our guests."

As they descended, Charlie looked at Julia: "I'll love you forever." He lowered his voice, smiled, and looked down at the twenty-third step. "And our stairs, and the wash stand, and your dresser..."

Julia tightened her grip on Charlie's arm. A joyful smile lit her face as she said, "I think it's time to paint all the columns on The Row white again."

"I'll talk to our neighbors tomorrow," Charlie said. "Tonight belongs to Drummer Boy, and to us."

EPILOGUE

On a night when the moon was full, Dattie Tucker was escorted to her white and gold carriage by a young man who knew how to handle the four white horses.

As she was helped into her carriage, Dattie turned to the driver, who was attired in Dattie's idea of livery which consisted of black trousers and a red jacket with a coat of arms featuring a large, gray, Persian cat. "Theo, please go first to the square so that I may lay catnip at the foot of Drummer Boy's statue, then just drive for a while." Dattie pulled her ermine coat around her and adjusted its hood over her curls.

"Yes ma'am," said Theo, who was fond of the old lady although he thought she should have been named Dotty instead of Dattie.

Dattie continued to see Sir Arthur, who bought Euphemia's house on The Row. He often accompanied his neighbor on her nocturnal rides which became longer and longer.

***

James built a smaller version of the Toombs' mansion on his property near Greenway Plantation. No one thought ill of the three little girls for treating both the original on The Row and the replica as their home. Dattie Tucker's carriage was always at the girls' disposal in the daytime since Dattie left her home only at night and only when the moon was full.

***

In a completely refurbished library off the square, Belle Irving surveyed a load of five hundred new books she was cataloging as a gift for the citizenry. Later that day, author Fanny Kemble reviewed her book, *Journal of a Residence on a Georgia Plantation*, for Washington library members. Fanny stayed on as a guest in Belle Irving's home until she left to take over the Butler Plantation. With Julia and Charlie's permission, Fanny took Lily with her. James Battle hired an overseer for his one hundred acres and joined her a few months later. Under James' management, the Butler Plantation became the most successful plantation in the South. The little girls had yet another home to add to their collection as well as another mother. Julia, Charlie, and the twins visited often. Sometimes the twins missed Lily so much they visited the Battle family without their parents.

***

Before James left, he and Charlie completed a small house for Tilde on the other side of the barn. It was built of prime Georgia wood and painted white like the other Row houses. While she was not technically on The Row, Tilde considered herself a resident. She sat on her front porch with a cat in her lap that had refused to go home after The Drummer Boy Ball where shrimp was served. The cat was gray.

"General," Tilde said to the cat as she stroked his fur, "we has seen it all."

***

The freedmen prospered from diligent dedication to properties of their own. They were mostly accepted in Georgia townships because of their reverence for the land. Many of the freedmen moved home from the North where they felt they weren't acceptable. Those who had remained were happy to share their unexpected, newfound prosperity.

***

Rolly Anderson bought a five thousand acre plantation in Taliaferro County next to Ibo's hundred acre plot. He built a wooden walkway between his columned mansion and Ibo's modest home. Every ten years, Rolly rebuilt the walkway.

***

Charlie was instrumental in the unwritten, backroom deal known as The Compromise of 1877 which agreed to the withdrawal of Union troops from the South in exchange for a Republican Congress. Charlie and Julia grew old together in the Toombs' mansion until Julia's death. Charlie was disconsolate over his loss. He became a recluse who never left the house. When his new neighbors on The Row dropped by to check on him, they always found him in one of the rockers by the fireplace, even in the summer.

***

In 1973, the Toombs' mansion was given to the state of Georgia and named a historic site. Docents often pointed to the crack in the marble top of the dresser, explaining that the fissure was caused when General Robert Toombs carried the marble top outside during a fire set by the KKK in retaliation for the General harboring a Mulatto child.

The dresser, with the top which cracked when it slipped to the ground, is one of the few pieces of original furniture, the docents noted. They also explained that Charles Irving was the last Confederate resident to live there until after Reconstruction ended. Following the death of his wife Julia, who was the former Mrs. Toombs, Charles gave some of the furniture to his three daughters, then sold most of what remained. For reasons known only to him, he kept a few pieces. Charles had an intense attachment to the dresser and washstand and found comfort in the rockers, all of which were rather worthless because of wear and damage.

AUTHOR'S NOTES

Love Rises is a post-bellum love story based on fact, but the romance is entirely a work of fiction created from old photographs and stories passed down in my family for generations, then coupled with my imagination. While the novel concerns actual persons and events, it is only a story. There was a Confederate General Robert Toombs. He had a beautiful wife named Julia and a favored neighbor, Lt. Charles E. Irving a.k.a Irvin, who was my ancestor. They lived in Washington, Georgia. Julia never posed for her portrait in the nude, and there is no proof of a love affair between the young lieutenant and the older Mrs. Toombs.

Shortly after the Civil War ended, Charlie saw the General, who was wanted for treason, through the picket lines to Mobile, then to New Orleans. From the port city, the older man sailed for exile in Paris. Before he left, he asked Charlie to look after Julia. It is also true that Charlie spent a great deal of time with Julia before she joined the General in Paris for a short visit, after which she returned home. This visit allows for fictional babies Lucy's and Paris' paternity to lie with either Charlie or the General.

General Toombs, still wanted for treason, made a pact with Union President Andrew Johnson. Although the General refused to ask for pardon and never swore allegiance to the United States, President Johnson generously granted him passage home to Washington, Georgia where the Toombs' mansion stood a short distance from Charlie Irving's residence on The Row.

Julia's letter to Charlie, to which she refers in the novel, is written on crested stationery. The letter is dated December 6, 1865, just before she sailed for Europe to join her husband. Here is a copy of her letter given to my mother and me by relatives in Washington, Georgia:

My dear Charlie,

How can I thank you for your devoted attention and kindness to my husband, I fail to know how to procede (sic.) — accept my love and good wishes for this present world and a home in Heaven at last — I send you Dear Charlie a box which I have prized, I give it to you because I love you—I intend it as a Christmas gift—put your collars, cravats -and pocket handkerchiefs in it to remember me—when in a far and distant land, where you was* so kind as to get my husband out of reach of these vile Yankees—I am so sorry I could not see you before I left—but fate has decreed it otherwise and I must be content with the past—God help

you always and ever is the prayer of your devoted and grateful friend.

Julia A. Toombs

* The use of the word *was* in Julia Toombs letter
was correct English usage in 1865.

On the back of the letter, Lieutenant Charles Irving
wrote this of Julia:

> Touch it not—let it be—main evidences of
> gratitude are so limited—appreciation for dis-
> interested services so small—that when one is
> found like the Authoress of the note—within,
> we touch our hat with reverence and bow to
> the sacred promptings of a grateful nature. CEI

***

As to the children in this novel, there was no Mulatto
child and the other two are fictional as well. History
lists two daughters and a son for General and Mrs.
Robert Toombs, although before his death, the colorful General admitted to four children in a *New York
Times* interview. He always swore a singular devotion
to his wife.

Fanny Kemble married and divorced Pierce Butler
but could never have married fictional character
James Battle. There is historical evidence that white
women were known to have sexual liaisons with
black men during the 1800's.

In a post-bellum family photograph album which I

inherited, there is a picture of a beautiful young woman dressed in purple velvet. On the back, in my grandmother's handwriting, the photo is labeled "Miss Jennie Toombs, daughter of Brig. General Robert Toombs of Georgia." The Toombs' daughters were named Louisa and Sallie. Their brother, Lawrence, died in infancy. The General's brother did have a daughter named Jenny. Perhaps my grandmother was mistaken with both the parentage and spelling of Jenny's name. I spent many hours looking at Jennie's photograph, and subsequently feel she gave me permission to imagine her as Lucy, the child of Charlie and Julia's fictional love affair. Also, I imagined that Julia's husband, Brigadier General Robert Augustus Toombs, approved of the affair and the child, because he left his home to Charlie in his will.

I coalesced the dates of births, deaths, and altered some incidents in order to make them fit the plot. I tried to present the spirit and the setting of those who suffered through the "War of Northern Aggression," as Southerners still say when they refer to the bloodiest war with the greatest number of casualties in U.S. military history. That Julia and Charlie found love during the harsh aftermath of war called Reconstruction is proof that love can defy circumstance and thrive in the midst of death and destruction.

My research would have been much more extensive and time consuming had I not felt free to call on my son-in-law, Dr. John Patrick Daly, who teaches history at State University of New York, Brockport. He answered my constant questions instantly, patiently, and accurately. A preview of his book, *Civil War II,* was of great help to me.

Love Rises

Bella's comments about pictures in the

FAMILY PHOTO ALBUM

Your affectionate Aunt, Mollie.

Aunt Mollie. Faraway in Alabama.

Is this the guy who was a Drummer Boy in the
Civil War? This isn't a Civil War uniform.

Dressed for a picnic.

Why so glum? You weren't supposed to smile for the camera then, but pleasant was acceptable.

Why didn't you sell that broach for cat food?

Where'd you get that hat? Or is it a hat?

Love Rises

Never hang on to a man with folded arms.

Bella Battle

Is this a Toombs' daughter or a Toombs' niece?
Great grandmother says she's a Toombs.

Maybe this is Fielding's first wife and Belle's sister who died young, leaving several small children.

Bella Battle

Is this Belle who told Fielding he could marry only her, and no other, after his wife's death? Belle was thought "too pretty to marry." She sacrificed her single state to wed her brother-in-law and raise her dead sister's children.

Is this glum at an older age?

This is Bella's great grandfather who might not have approved of *Love Rises*.

Is this Belle's sister and Fielding's first wife?

This may be Fielding.
Can he handle Belle?

Aunt Dattie never married. She took care of the household and cracked all the china secreted from Sherman's March to the Sea. When the bread was passed, she always said, "I'll take the end crust."

Don't know who you are, but you have an impos-
ing mustache.

She looks feisty enough to be Lily.

Sweet Pea.

Is that a rabbit under your shirt?
What are you pointing at?

Sewanee, affectionately known as S'wee.
Must be from Tennessee, not to be confused with
the river in Florida..

Is this Belle's sister, too?

The family buggy. Is That Lily in front?
Who's inside?

Love Rises

Maribelle, born many years after the Civil War.

Everyone wondered if Mab would find a husband.
She was picky.

Is this Lucy?

Is this Paris? She doesn't look like a twin.

What are you doing here, Bella?
You're too young to be in this album.

Bella Battle

This may be Fielding and Belle after a few years of
marriage. Who's in charge?
Seated Fielding or Standing Belle?

Could this be Euphemia?

---

*~~ For photographs of General Robert Toombs and his
wife Julia Toombs, search online ~~*

DEAR READER

Thanks for taking the time to read Love Rises. If you enjoyed the book, I would really appreciate, your rating and/or review on Amazon, Goodreads, and any other book-related websites.

See Bella Battle Romance and Mysteries page on Facebook for coming releases.

ABOUT THE AUTHOR

Bella Battle lives with her cat, Drummer Boy, north of the Mason Dixon line where she devotes herself to writing romance and mystery novels. She relies heavily on Granny Battle.

www.ingramcontent.com/pod-product-compliance
Lightning Source LLC
Chambersburg PA
CBHW031338040426
42443CB00006B/386